Sweet Nothings

AN ANTHOLOGY

Sweet

OF **ROCK AND ROLL**

Nothings

IN AMERICAN POETRY

Edited, with an Introduction,
by **Jim Elledge**

Indiana University Press

BLOOMINGTON AND INDIANAPOLIS

The paper used in this publication meets the minimum requirements of Amer-
ican National Standard for Information Sciences—Permanence of Paper for
Printed Library Materials, ANSI Z39.48-1984.

MANUFACTURED IN THE UNITED STATES OF AMERICA

Library of Congress Cataloging-in-Publication Data

Sweet nothings : an anthology of rock and roll in American poetry /
    edited, with an introduction, by Jim Elledge.
        p.   cm.
    Includes bibliographical references and index.
    ISBN 0-253-31936-6
    1. Rock music—Poetry. 2. American poetry—20th century.
I. Elledge, Jim, date.
PS595.R57S94   1994
811'.54080357—dc 20

                                                    93-11795

1 2 3 4 5 00 99 98 97 96 95 94

To Michael David Hubbard these words:

Teach your parents well
Their children's hell. . . .

The introduction of novel fashions in music is a thing to beware of as endangering the whole fabric of society whose most important conventions are unsettled by any revolution in that quarter.

—Plato

A wop bop a loo mop a lop bam boom!
—Little Richard, "Tutti-Frutti"

Contents

[x]

[xii]

Introduction
Rock and Roll and American Poetry

In the early, hip-swiveling days of rock and roll, more of American society deemed the new music an embarrassing nuisance, if not an outright sin, than recognized the tunes of, say, Bill Haley as an emerging genre of popular music. However, once the then-fledgling record industry discovered that a poor white boy from Tupelo, Mississippi, decked out in cat clothes and crowned with a sky-high pompadour, could siphon exorbitant amounts of money from the post–World War II prosperity U.S. teenagers enjoyed simply by warbling about hound dogs and blue suede shoes while writhing onstage in an unabashedly sexual manner, it bowed before the King.

At the same time, other facets of American capitalism, also dazzled by the King's gold lamé suit aglow among hordes of teens and young adults, paid homage to rock and roll. Hollywood offered adolescents *The Blackboard Jungle,* which featured on its soundtrack "Rock around the Clock," perhaps the first rock and roll hit with a "message"; guest shots of rockers cranking on flicks like *The Girl Can't Help It*; and hours of Frankie and Annette crooning while cavorting, frame after frame, through various beach-blanket escapades. TV gave prime-time exposure to Ozzie and Harriet Nelson's heartthrob son Ricky, who became one of a number of teen idols; to *American Bandstand,* the progenitor of hype; and to *The Ed Sullivan Show,* Sunday evening's "wholesome" entertainment—lion tamers from West Germany, Perry Como solos, and the bons mots of cute-to-kill puppet-mouse Topo Gigio—occasionally elbow to elbow with rockers. However, more open to rock and roll than the silver screen and more focused on rock and roll than the boob tube, Top Forty AM radio offered the disembodied but riveting round-the-clock patter of Alan Freed, Bob "Wolfman Jack" Smith, and numerous other DJs, spinning new platters late into the night, spreading the word—which was the beat.

Most chroniclers date the birth of rock and roll to 1955, the year in which Bill Haley and His Comets' "Rock around the Clock" sky-rocketed out of *The Blackboard Jungle* onto the pop charts, where it remained at Number One for twenty-four consecutive weeks.[1] This watershed event heralded the arrival in American society at large of a new consumer and a new music: teenagers and rock and roll. Suddenly, the captains of American capitalism realized that each had a money-making potential neither had previously possessed on such a large scale and offered both a new status—visibility.

Aficionados less interested in its popular acceptance and its money-making potential than intrigued by its spirit and by the evolution of its music, presentation, and lyric content have traced rock and roll's origins to earlier decades, citing the blues, country-western, and gospel as its roots. In fact, most readily agree that these three genres of music are simply "modern" versions of ancient, African musics.

Indeed, songs with titles suggestive of the "new" fifties music have been a part of American culture since at least 1922, when Trixie Smith recorded "My Daddy Rocks Me with One Steady Roll." A number of recordings with similar titles were to be heard in the two decades which followed: Bob Robinson's "Rocking and Rolling" (1930), the Boswell Sisters' "Rock and Roll" (1934), Buddy Jones's "Rockin' Rollin' Mama" (1939), and Wild Bill Moore's "We're Gonna Rock, We're Gonna Roll" (1947).[2] Some musicologists insist it was Moore's song which "inspired" Alan Freed to dub the new wave of popular tunes *rock and roll*.[3] Rock critic Robert Palmer has identified Joe Washington Brown and Austin Coleman's version of "Run, Old Jeremiah," recorded in 1934 by John and Alan Lomax, as prototypical rock and roll, and anyone lucky enough to have heard this "folk" song would be hard put to dispute his view.[4]

Regardless of when rock and roll began, the fact remains that the artists who followed the original rockers took what characteristics they could or wanted from their predecessors, added different instrumentation or lyric content to the music, and were, a few years later, overshadowed by another wave of singers, musicians, and lyricists who changed the music in *their* way so that it became a *new* genre. Versions of what each up-and-coming rocker made from what he or she had heard as rock and roll were replaced by his or her version of it, which was replaced by the next rocker's, and so on for more than three decades. Thus, the girl group sound, the phenomenon of teen idols, the Mersey beat, acid rock, the San Francisco, Texas, and New Orleans sounds, soul, surf, TexMex, garage music, folk-rock, disco, reggae, glitter rock, punk, funk, techno-pop, and New Wave—each a variety of music aired over AM and FM radio stations to millions of listeners during the past thirty years—have risen from previous genres of rock and roll, given rock and roll new sounds, techniques, and concerns, remained in the spotlight for a time, then disappeared, subsumed into or overwhelmed by the type of music that followed. In a few years, we'll see that even rap, heavy metal, and alternative music—current crazes—will have followed this pattern.

In one way or another, all forms of rock and roll owe their existence to a handful of primarily but not exclusively southern, male performers who sang of that little home-wrecker "Long, Tall Sally," of their favorite article of clothing, a pair of "Blue Suede Shoes," of a jailhouse that rocked, of the elusive "Maybelline," or knew, prophetically as it turned out, that there was "a whole lotta shakin' goin' on." Once begun, that "shakin'" would never stop. While in 1958 Danny and the Juniors were confident that "rock and roll [was] here to stay," more than two decades later, Billy Joel surveyed the multifaceted music scene that surrounded him and decided, "It's still rock and roll to me."

Moreover, despite comments to the contrary, rock and roll spoke to (perhaps *shouted about* is more accurate) teenage concerns. In the Coasters' "Yakety-Yak," it complained about what so-and-so's parents tend to be. In the Everly Brothers' "Wake Up, Little Susie," it consoled those fearful of getting an undeserved bad rep and being grounded for at least life. In Elvis Presley's "Heartbreak Hotel," it mapped a territory crowded with the jilted. In Jerry Lee Lewis's "High School Confidential," it agreed that school's a bummer.

Things haven't changed all that much since rock and roll's early days. In fact, the only difference between the mid-fifties and the early nineties is that showcases for rock and roll are now more numerous and widespread (AM *and* FM radio stations, MTV, etc.), not only because rock and roll has grown into a billion-dollar industry but also because the Baby Boomers of the 1950s, who often spent every cent of their allowances on Top Ten hits, have grown into salary-earning adults with an affinity for the music that has been an integral part of their lives for more than three decades. They may not know the difference between the groups EIEIO, INXS, and OMD, but they'll never forget the tune Gene Pitney or Brenda Lee or Paul Anka was singing over the car radio or on the hi-fi at the magic moment of their first kiss. Aware not only of the music's popularity and profit-generating potential among both the younger generation and—because of its value as fodder for nostalgia—the older generation, Big Business uses rock and roll on TV and radio commercials as background music and hires has-beens or current superstars as product-endorsers to hustle everything from scooters to soda pop to high-top sneakers to laundry detergent. Because TV and radio, and the commercials which support both, are everywhere, rock and roll now permeates our culture.

Rock and roll has been subsumed much less obviously, but no less zealously, by another facet of U.S. culture—by *poetry*—and for the same reason that capitalism borrowed it. Many of the poets now achieving recognition, or on the verge of it, are those Baby Boomers who adored Elvis, spent their lawn-mowing and baby-sitting money on his 45s and LPs, stood in line for hours to see his flicks, felt betrayed when he enlisted in the army then joy when he was discharged, and abandoned him for someone else when the British invaded the U.S. in February 1964.

Because rock and roll played an integral, often all-consuming, role in their "formative years" (to borrow a phrase from an early Wonder Bread TV commercial), no one should be surprised that the music appears in the work of many of the Baby Boom poets, especially in their poems dealing with adolescence and young adulthood. Often serving as backdrop to particular remembered experiences, creating specific moods, or existing as a part of the poet's psychic landscape, the elements of rock and roll incorporated into their poetry may have symbolic values as well, reflecting certain cultural norms, serving as codes for particular situations, and almost always representing a time of innocence—or an era of innocence turned sour. Like rock and roll, the poems included in *Sweet Nothings* cover many topics, from the personal to the sociopolitical, from the historical to the contemporary: first love, the problems that arise between parents and children, the conflict between conformity and individuality, rebellion against authority of all types, the injustices of our society and the world at large, bigotry on all levels, the desire to live a rewarding life, and always the paeans dedicated to particular rock artists—some superstars, others virtually unknown except by a handful of fans.

Undoubtedly, rock and roll has influenced the poets included in *Sweet Nothings* in other, more subtle ways than simply thematically. We could argue convincingly that, as they were growing up, the poets heard rock and roll lyrics more often than they read poetry, and so learned many of the basics of poetry writing from it because a large percentage of rock and roll lyrics employ the techniques of writing traditionally associated with poetry: rhyme, metaphor, imagery, allusion, etc. We need only look at lyrics written or sung by the best of rock and roll's performers—from Smokey Robinson to Martin L. Gore, from Carl Perkins and Buddy Holly to Paul Simon and Joni Mitchell to They Might Be Giants and Queen Latifah—to see poetry's relationship to rock and roll lyrics. Indeed, Bob Dylan's lyrics serve better than anyone's as an example of that relationship.

If the published "facts" of Bob Dylan's life contain any truth at all, his songs, *the* most "literary" of all lyrics, add an ironic twist to the influence rock and roll seems to have had on U.S. poets. It's relatively obvious that Dylan was not only influenced by, but borrowed heavily from, the themes and techniques of the poetry of the modernist masters—particularly T. S. Eliot and Ezra Pound—as well as the French surrealists. By incorporating elements and techniques of their work into his lyrics, he in turn offered the adolescents and young adults who played his LPs, specifically those from *Another Side of Bob Dylan* to *Blonde on Blonde*, what he had learned from modernism and surrealism. (It's also obvious that some of Dylan's earlier songs were heavily influenced by poetry. The structure of his "A Hard Rain's A-Gonna Fall," for example, is based on the English ballad "Lord Randall.") The fans who spent hours listening to and interpreting his lyrics—and who would later become today's poets—were undoubtedly influenced by him to some degree, consciously or not.

However, it is virtually impossible to ascertain the influence rock and roll has had on the poets included here. Readers interested in such questions should consult the "Contributors' Notes and Comments" section, in which the poets were given the opportunity to discuss the relationship of their poems included in this anthology to rock and roll. The comments they offered are often eye-opening.

Arranged in a loosely thematic manner, *Sweet Nothings* is meant to mirror the varied music that rock and roll has evolved into during its four-decade existence. Its poems are not rock and roll lyrics, but works of literary merit in which one genre or another of rock and roll plays a part, whether overtly or subtly.

Some poems don't focus on a genre of rock and roll per se but on its predecessors which, during various times in rock and roll's history, have been acknowledged as important to and recorded by some of its best performers. The Rolling Stones and Janis Joplin built formidable careers on the blues, Bob Dylan's *Nashville Skyline* and the Byrds' *Sweetheart of the Rodeo* are rock and roll *and* country-western classics, and any soul, funk, or rap artist from Aretha Franklin and Otis Redding to Prince and Hammer owes an inestimable debt to gospel. Indeed, all performers from Elvis Presley to Elvis Costello to the Elvis Brothers and beyond have simply sung that combination of blues, country-western, and gospel loosely labeled *rock and roll*.

NOTES

1. Joel Whitburn, *The Billboard Book of Top 40 Hits* (New York: Billboard, 1985), p. 147.

2. Dave Marsh and Kevin Stein, *The Book of Rock Lists* (New York: Dell, 1981), pp. 180–181.

3. Ibid., p. 181.

4. Robert Palmer, "Rock Begins," in *The Rolling Stone Illustrated History of Rock and Roll*, ed. Jim Miller, rev. ed. (New York: Random, 1980), p. 3.

Sweet Nothings

DAVID WOJAHN

W.C.W. Watching Presley's Second Appearance on *The Ed Sullivan Show:* Mercy Hospital, Newark, 1956

The tube,
      like the sonnet,
            is a fascist form.
I read they refused
        to show this kid's
            wriggling bum.
"The pure products
        of America . . ."
            etc.
From Mississippi!
       Tupelo,
          a name like a flower
you wouldn't want
        beside you
           in a room
like this,
      where the smells hold you
            a goddamn
hostage to yourself,
        where talk's
          no longer cheap.
Missed connections,
        missed connections—
          a junk heap

blazing there in
                    Ironbound,
                              a couple kids
beside it,
              juiced on the
                              cheapest wine. Mid-
thought. Midwinter,
                    and stalled
                              between the TV screen
and window. . . .
                    This pomped-up kid,
                              who preens
and tells us
              "Don't Be Cruel."
                              Kid, forget it.
You don't know
                    a fucking thing
                              about cruelty yet.

NEAL BOWERS

On the Elvis Mailing List

It started with the Greatest Hits album,
ordered one night in a haze
of nostalgia and wine, toll-free
in the middle of *Notorious*, just after
Claude Raines started poisoning Ingrid Bergman.

In a room at the top of a long
flight of stairs she was weakening,
thinking all the while how much she
wanted, needed, and loved Cary Grant,
who was taking too long to understand
it was now or never.

By the time he rescued her,
our album was being processed
somewhere in New Jersey, and we were
already in line for motorcoach
tours to Graceland, porcelain busts,
and an opportunity to give, tax-free,
to the Presley Trauma Center.

Everything worked out well,
except for Claude Raines, of course,
who was taken inside behind a heavy door
by two men who would laugh at anyone
wailing "Don't be cruel."

ROBERT GIBB

Letter to Russell Barron

Most likely whatever glimpse we caught
Of each other will turn out

To have been the last one.
I don't know where a solitary one of you

Are, or even if you are all alive.
Much as I might like it

I don't believe I'll ever make it back
To sit in Chiodo's drinking beer

Just down the street from WAMO,
Or that the currents are going

To carry me home. Russell,
You're the one who turned me round

To rhythm-and-blues, 45's with labels
Luminescent as tropical plants.

I can't tell you all that they've meant.
Without them

I might never have reached Muddy Waters,
Hank Crawford, or those horses

Cantering along the keyboard
In Tatum's deft and stately hands.

If you made it over the river
I hope you got farther than the suburbs.

[4]

That evening I was terrified by your father
Bulling his bulk into the furniture,

Drunk and wheezing like a narrow-gauge
There on the living room floor—

I barely knew the first thing about singing.
Listen, Russell, wherever you are

I hope that from time to time
You rise up in the heart of your house

In the soft, mammal dark.
I hope you have a woman like I do

Who hasn't contracted terminal good taste.
I'm sorry about the way we lose one another

Along our drift of days,
That the trolleys have vanished

Along with the Mystery Train.
And I'm sorry about the Friday

I never showed up.
I was with that lovely armful of lonely bones,

Skinny Margie Stulginski,
And I'd most likely do so again.

DAVID WOJAHN

Woody Guthrie Visited by Bob Dylan: Brooklyn State Hospital, New York, 1961

He has lain here for a terrible, motionless
Decade, and talks through a system of winks
And facial twitches. The nurse props a cigarette
Between his lips, wipes his forehead. She thinks
He wants to send the kid away, but decides
To let him in—he's waited hours.
Guitar case, jean jacket. A corduroy cap slides
Down his forehead. Doesn't talk. He can't be more
Than twenty. He straps on the harmonica holder,
Tunes up, and begins his "Song to Woody,"
Trying to sound three times his age, sandpaper
Dustbowl growl, the song interminable, inept. Should he
Sing another? The eyes roll their half-hearted yes.
The nurse grits her teeth, stubs out the cigarette.

DOROTHY BARRESI

Late Summer News

Applications are now being
accepted for private burning.
—Radio Announcement,
Charlotte, NC

Come over here from over there, girl.
—Bob Dylan

Up and down this red clay route
where heat makes waves, mailboxes
hold a stiff salute above the chokeweed:
today, against all odds
someone has remembered you.
My hand tests the little oven.
Visa, J.C. Penney, what I owe
bakes to a nothing loaf of flatbread and salt.
These mornings I confess
I'm happy to find bills there
or anything else that bears my name
plain as light through a wax paper window.
Starved, I'll take these words in gulps.
"Pledge to the Radical Gay Alliance,"
"Plant a tree in Israel,"
even the stacked deck of people's needs
I read lovingly, repeat
each return address for my mantra.
Then this: smaller
than the white-shrouded others, an envelope
from a friend who writes for nothing I can give.
J&L Steel turns the air orange, she says

in the old neighborhood;
bag ladies shamble up and down
Murray Avenue, still speaking to the personal angels
that live in their coat pockets,
and caged live chickens
bask in Neederman's doorway, waiting to be delivered
unto the butcher and the rabbi.
"What I mean most
is that laughter isn't the same without you."
Her daughter, she closes, has grown gorgeous
and last month married for love.

Who knows what to wish for.
The big picture hides in its own wide margins—
no one sees it, or why
we sign our names to each day that comes
wearing its new-wave fashions.
This time, when the white parachute of memory
blooms backward from the letter in my hand
I'm ready for it, am meant to see
projected in its pure, billowing center
how the blind really do lead us. There:
my father in his catcher's squat
in 1946, a Tareyton dangling from his lips—
his slow loopy charm.
My mother at Sacred Heart High
taking lessons in resisting charm, fingers crossed.
My Italian grandfather kneeling
to his 80th garden, basil, fennel, chard,
my Irish grandfather's cancer
thriving like a wrong note in his vocal cords.
Friends, I see them, too,
playing air guitars and clinking bottles of Iron City
against Mouton Rothschild, 1978.
If choices were wood
I could build a bridge back to them

with the choices I've made to be here.
I could burn one down.
Standing here watching, head tilted, I think
how I must look for all the world
like that RCA dog, full of sweet, dopey trust.
The gravel makes a noise under my feet
like just-thrown dice, and
what silk there is floats away from me
over hundred-year pines,
all the bright strings attached.

RACHEL LODEN

"Tumbling Dice"

I thought all your walled cities
would fall
to rock & roll,
I thought no suffering was safe
when Smokey sang.
If Otis
could not teach you tenderness—
Aretha sweet love—
then I was wrong.

Do roses push
up through the streets
of Spanish Harlem,
is "Ooo Baby Baby"
still the melting point of ice?
Will we always find
some rooftop we can drift on
to the roll of the tumbling dice,
sweet darling
the roll of the tumbling dice. . . .

Jungle Music

My father yelled, "Turn that damn thing down!"
That thing was the mahogany RCA hi-fi console
with a ten ounce mono arm my parents tried to save
for *Oklahoma* and The Jackie Gleason Orchestra.
"Jungle music" meant the big black stack of 45's
I bought, one a week, 79¢ at Wilmington Dry Goods—
the only thing I'd work ten minutes for
my old man said.

It wasn't Chuck's fault, or Fats' or even Little Richard's.
Black kids only taught us how to fight, or run.
No one let us watch them dance.
It was Mrs. Coombs who taught the beat
and how to move. Sixth grade dancing class at the Legion Hall
aimed for social graces. She frowned,
watching us stumble through the fox trots, tangos
and waltzes, but when it was time to jitterbug
and she slipped on "Maybe Baby" we learned the steps
and begged for more. Mrs. Coombs, you accidentally led
the Rock and Roll Revolution out of the ghettos
and rockabilly roadhouses into Woodstown, New Jersey.

I hope you're proud. We were. At last
we knew we wouldn't have to wear our parents' Doris Day,
Tommy Dorsey or Tony Bennett shoes.
We had Bobby Day, Lee Dorsey, Joe Bennett and the Sparkletones,
tan shoes, pink shoelaces, white bucks and black slax.
At party after party we got high on Coke and Luckies

[11]

and bopped until our loafers cracked and sweaty hands
slid apart. We knew every crack in every half-flat basement floor
in town. St. Joseph's, 1st Presbyterian and Woodstown High
gave us room to run away.

All day we slaved in class to beat the Russians to the moon.
All night we studied for our black belts in Rock.
If we couldn't get a date, a car or a drink,
the radio always answered our prayers, pushed the message
deep behind enemy lines. We danced in parking lots and in cars,
four in the front, singing, swaying and snapping our fingers
to Hy Lit and Joe Niagra, trying to do 100 and live to tell,
one eye on the lookout for Dead Man's Curve, double or nothing.
On Sundays we found 100 watt black gospel shows wailing
with the Rev. Cleveland, Muntz TV and combination screen
and storm window deals.

It was 1957. The only flower children sold poppies
on Veteran's Day. Love was something we'd find
after we screwed the Kramer sisters. How could there be peace?
The generation gap widened into no-man's land
and we had leaders more bullet-proof than John Wayne.
Frankie Lymon, Richie Valens, Little Willie John, Buddy Holly,
Chuck Willis and Sam Cooke would fight forever.
Bad meant good. Tough meant better. It was Daddy Cool
Reet Petite and Gone.

But Teen Angel brought real death. Planes crashed. Cars burned.
Drugs we'd never heard of snapped hearts like worn-out E-strings.
The resistance got real gone.
Alan Freed got busted. Dick Clark got younger and richer.
Phil Spector hid behind a wall of sound
and speed killed cats who didn't even own a car.
Our parents did the twist in go-go clubs
and we lost the British Invasion, hopelessly hating the Beatles.

Someone bought our songs and we didn't get a cent.
Someone killed our gods and we didn't see the trial.
Someone started a war for us, and made us fight.
Someone yelled come home, but we were dancing in the night.

THOMAS REITER

Class Bully

Pursued by one nun or another
in loop after loop through the cloakroom,
the desk globe wobbling in your slipstream,
you were determined to go straight
to hell, so they made an example of you
to save our souls. That time the principal
made us pray for you, we burned:
you washed our faces in snow, all of us
in one recess to set the kind of record
you prized, like being twice held back.
Still we gathered around you and learned
what an apple corking the tailpipe
of the scout leader's Buick could do.
One night you knocked down the fence
surrounding the shell of the new convent
and led us through the front door.
Lines of uprights marked interior walls,
so we ghosted into cloistered lives
vivid as holy pictures of saints in cells.
Next a stairway to floorless beams
and a view over school grounds to the river,
where a searchlight scanned the channel
for buoys marking sandbars as
a towboat pushed against the current, bound
for where kids always gathered
to see those barges riding low with coal
lock through the dam into port.

Caught here, we'd be included with you
in the pastor's Lenten sermon:
barges bank to bank upriver and down
and for all eternity that tonnage
rattling burning onto our heads.
Under the open rooftree and rafters
we followed you, arms outstretched,
heel-and-toe along the center beam,
faking false moves as though
you could make another beam miraculously
receive our first step in air. Today
I learned you are the first of us
to die, lost when your parachute failed
during war games, and I remembered
the day you held us in a circle
because Mother Superior had given you
the sexton's duty of ringing us in
for daily mass. Right there on the diamond
you reached for a bell rope from the sky
and bent your back to show us
how to time the notes, their proper rise and fall.
Filing in next morning, we called for
a steeple version of "Rock Around the Clock"
that would put you into your cloakroom stride,
but instead you sounded over our heads
the long boredom of morality,
so that afterwards it was nothing to become
crossing guard, your white belt and raised hand
keeping us from going under the wheels.

PAUL ZARZYSKI

How Near Vietnam Came to Us

The ID bracelet I never did give
my first girl friend cost me more
than I'd ever spent before on love
for anything but beer. We sipped
cherry cokes to nickel-a-hit
Rolling Stones' "Let's spend the night
together," "Paint it black," "Time
is on my side," and "I can't get no
satisfaction." I wanted her eyes gleaming
my gold surprise—one small touch
from diamond—something to sanctify
going all the way, something I hoped
would stave off the ultimate pain
all love comes to
without warning. We both went cold
against the mix of malt shop rollick,
the carhop motioning her
to the telephone news from a TV war
forced home too real—everything
in our teenage, red-Chev niche
eclipsed to this foreign dark:
an eight-day fire fight,
some napalmed hill of jungle
dubbed in numbers, her brother
tallied to the MIA. His name
stamped in cheap metal
instantly meant more than all

the earth's elegance—romantic verse
of rock-'n'-roll inscribed in gold—
more than any purple-hearted Requiem
a red, white, and blue
united world or I could ever give.

WALTER MCDONALD

The Songs We Fought For

We drank while half the stars came out for us,
Willie and Waylon, Jane and Loretta,
ours in the glow of the jukebox.

Over the laughter and smoke of local
men and women groping for their lives,
they sob-sang all we hoped to know

of lonesome love. Nothing like
honky-tonk songs could break a man's heart
with the draft and a war in Vietnam

drawing him closer daily. We slumped
under our Stetsons, squinting
in blue smoke layered like gunfire,

and bought pitchers of beer for women
we never hoped to marry. Each time I took
Sweet Darlin's hand and led her

onto the dance floor, I felt the world
should end like that, slow-dancing
close as we'd ever be to another in clothes,

lost in a sad, sweet fiddle-rhythm,
sliding on polished boots
and humming softly to ourselves.

SIDNEY BURRIS

Very True Confessions

Once, I grew long hair
in a town with a Howitzer
parked in the town square.
I didn't want to want to belong.

Not that I was odd.
I shot up gangly
and light-headed
as milkweed and pod,

saw Vietnam in black and white
at six o'clock on eight
(with highlights at eleven),
stayed home a lot,

but attended the riots
that skewered our school,
and played enough football
to appease the poster

of Gayle Sayers I'd hung
like an icon
on the wall. Every night
the same old thing:

rather than Latin,
I'd translate myself
hurdling into a heaven
of stars, or else

sneak a beer and cut
the music up, lie
down and wait
for Hendrix to appear

exhausted, wearied
by his burning guitar,
and then I'd slip
into a funk, a regular

guy blind-sided
by the world.
Concerned as I was,
I'd have sooner died
than go to bed
on time. It was 1969. Hell,
anywhere at all
was somewhere else instead.

YUSEF KOMUNYAKAA

Hanoi Hannah

Ray Charles! His voice
calls from waist-high grass,
& we duck behind gray sandbags.
"Hello, Soul Brothers. Yeah,
Georgia's also on my mind."
Flares bloom over the trees.
"Here's Hannah again.
Let's see if we can't
light her goddamn fuse
this time." Artillery
shells carve a white arc
against dusk. Her voice rises
from a hedgerow on our left.
"It's Saturday night in the States.
Guess what your woman's doing tonight.
I think I'll let Tina Turner
tell you, you homesick GIs."
Howitzers buck like a herd
of horses behind concertina.
"You know you're dead men,
don't you? You're dead
as King today in Memphis.
Boys, you're surrounded by
General Tran Do's division."
Her knife-edge song cuts
deep as a sniper's bullet.
"Soul Brothers, what you dying for?"

We lay down a white-klieg
trail of tracers. Phantom jets
fan out over the trees.
Artillery fire zeros in.
Her voice grows flesh
& we can see her falling
into words, a bleeding flower
no one knows the true name for.
"You're lousy shots, GIs."
Her laughter floats up
as though the airways are
buried under our feet.

MARK DEFOE

Forgetting the Sixties

Recall how she lolly-gagged beneath
kite-spangled skies at the big be-in,
then gave herself because naked kids
tossed frisbees and sunbeams lingered on
amber waves of hair. Sweetly stoned, she
gave herself to this really decent guy
who had planted daisies in rifles,
had smiled when the pigs wailed on his head.

Remember the clenched fist and shaken fist.
Remember flames eating flags eating flesh.
Remember Willie Peter dining
on palm-thatch. And slogan on slogan
and shouting until words surrendered
and what mattered limped on ahead—alone.

Leave it all, Leave it all, there behind
the black marble wall, built for the war
that failed us. Yet let the names come through,
names of the marchers and the marched upon.
(and who will now dare say which was which?)
Names from Watts and Detroit and Tet. Names
from Woodstock and Ohio. The names
of all who danced on mines, and who swam
the clay beneath Mississippi ponds.

Let them through, riding the reverbs, shades
of kids who worshiped Wayne and Gandhi.
Let them through on a wild raunchy riff,

shaking their locks. Let them boogie through,
dreaming smoke, dreaming stern drums, dreaming
dark riderless horses, dreaming boots
reversed in the stirrups, while Jimi
wrenches from his wailing strings again,
again, his final question—Oh, say
can you see? Oh, say, Oh, say, Oh, say,
Can you see? Can you see? Can You See?

DAVID TRINIDAD

Meet the Supremes

When Petula Clark sang "Downtown," I wished I
could go there with her. I wanted to be free
to have fun and fall in love, but from suburbia
the city appeared more distant and dangerous
than it actually was. I withdrew and stayed
in my room, listened to Jackie DeShannon sing
"What the World Needs Now Is Love." I agreed,
but being somewhat morose considered the song
a hopeless plea. I listened to Skeeter Davis'
"The End of the World" and decided that was
what it would be when I broke up with my first
boyfriend. My head spun as fast as the singles
I saved pennies to buy: "It's My Party," "Give
Him a Great Big Kiss," "(I Want to Be) Bobby's
Girl," "My Guy"—the list goes on. At the age
of ten, I rushed to the record store to get
"Little" Peggy March's smash hit, "I Will Follow
Him." An extreme example of lovesick devotion,
it held down the top spot on the charts for
several weeks in the spring of 1963. "Chapel
of Love" came out the following year and was
my favorite song for a long time. The girls
who recorded it, The Dixie Cups, originally
called themselves Little Miss & The Muffets.
They cut three hits in quick succession, then
disappeared. I remember almost the exact moment
I heard "Johnny Angel" for the first time: it

came on the car radio while we were driving
down to Laguna Beach to visit some friends of
the family. In the back seat, I set the book I'd
been reading beside me and listened, completely
mesmerized by Shelley Fabares' dreamy, teenage
desire. Her sentimental lyrics continue to move
me (although not as intensely) to this day.
Throughout adolesence, no other song affected me quite like that one.
On my transistor, I listened to the Top Twenty
countdown as, week after week, more girl singers and groups
came and went than I could keep track of:
  Darlene Love,
  Brenda Lee,
  Dee Dee Sharp,
  Martha Reeves
  & The Vandellas,
  The Chantels,
  The Shirelles,
  The Marvelettes,
  The Ronettes,
  The Girlfriends,
  The Rag Dolls,
  The Cinderellas,
  Alice Wonderland,
  Annette, The
  Beach-Nuts, Nancy
  Sinatra, Little
  Eva, Veronica,
  The Pandoras,
  Bonnie & The
  Treasures,
  The Murmaids,
  Evie Sands,
  The Pussycats,
  The Patty Cakes,
  The Trans-Sisters,

The Pixies Three,
The Toys, The
Juliettes and
The Pirouettes,
The Charmettes,
The Powder Puffs,
Patti Lace &
The Petticoats,
The Rev-Lons,
The Ribbons,
The Fashions,
The Petites,
The Pin-Ups,
Cupcakes,
Chic-Lets,
Jelly Beans,
Cookies, Goodies,
Sherrys, Crystals,
Butterflys,
Bouquets,
Blue-Belles,
Honey Bees,
Dusty Springfield,
The Raindrops,
The Blossoms,
The Petals,
The Angels,
The Halos,
The Hearts,
The Flamettes,
The Goodnight
Kisses, The
Strangeloves,
and The Bitter
Sweets.

I was ecstatic when "He's So Fine" hit the #1 spot.
I couldn't get the lyrics out of my mind and continued
to hum "Doo-lang Doo-lang Doo-lang" long after
puberty ended, a kind of secret anthem. Although
The Chiffons tried to repeat their early success
with numerous singles, none did as well as their
first release. "Sweet Talkin' Guy" came close,
sweeping them back into the Top Ten for a short
time, but after that there were no more hits.
Lulu made her mark in the mid-sixties with "To Sir with Love,"
which I would put on in order to daydream about
my junior high algebra instructor. By then I was
a genuine introvert. I'd come home from school,
having been made fun of for carrying my textbooks
like a girl, and listen to song after song from
my ever-expanding record collection. In those
days, no one sounded sadder than The Shangri-Las.
Two pairs of sisters from Queens, they became famous
for the classic "death disc shocker," "Leader of the Pack,"
and for their mod look. They were imitated (but never equaled)
by such groups as the Nu-Luvs and The Whyte Boots.
The Shangri-Las stayed on top for a couple of
years, then lost their foothold and split up.
Much later, they appeared on rock 'n' roll revival
shows, an even sadder act since Marge, the fourth
member of the band, had died of an accidental
drug overdose. I started smoking cigarettes around
this time, but wouldn't discover pills, marijuana
or alcohol until my final year of high school.
I loved Lesley Gore because she was always crying
and listened to "As Tears Go By" till the single had
so many scratches I couldn't play it anymore.
I preferred Marianne Faithful to The Beatles and
The Rolling Stones, was fascinated by the stories
about her heroin addiction and suicide attempt.
She's still around. So is Diana Ross. She made

it to superstardom alone, maintaining the success
she'd previously achieved as the lead singer of
The Supremes, one of the most popular girl groups
of all time. Their debut album was the first LP
I owned. Most of the songs on it were hits—
one would reach the top of the charts as another
hit the bottom. Little did I know, as I listened
to "Nothing but Heartaches" and "Where Did Our Love
Go," that nearly twenty years later I would hit
bottom in an unfurnished Hollywood single, drunk
and stoned and fed up, still spinning those same
old tunes. The friction that already existed
within The Supremes escalated in 1967 as Diana
Ross made plans for her solo career. The impending
split hit Florence the hardest. Rebelliously,
she gained weight and missed several performances,
and was finally told to leave the group. The pain
she experienced in the years that followed was
a far cry from the kind of anguish expressed
in The Supremes' greatest hits. Florence lost
the lawsuit she filed against Motown, failed at
a solo career of her own, went through a bitter
divorce, and ended up on welfare. In this classic
photograph of the group, however, Florence is
smiling. Against a black backdrop, she and Mary
look up at and frame Diana, who stands in profile
and raises her right hand, as if toward the future.
The girls' sequined and tasseled gowns sparkle
as they strike dramatic poses among some Grecian
columns. Thus, The Supremes are captured forever
like this, in an unreal, silvery light. That
moment, they're in heaven. Then, at least for Flo,
begins the long and painful process of letting go.

THOM GUNN

Painkillers

The King of rock 'n roll
grown pudgy, almost matronly,
Fatty in gold lamé,
mad King encircled
by a court of guards, suffering
delusions about assassination,
obsessed by guns, fearing
rivalry and revolt

popping his skin
with massive hits of painkiller

dying at 42.

What was the pain?
Pain had been the colours
of the bad boy with the sneer.

The story of pain, of separation,
was the divine comedy
he had translated
from black into white.

For white children too
the act of naming the pain
unsheathed
a keen joy at the heart of it.

Here they are still!
the disobedient

who keep a culture alive
by subverting it, turning
for example a subway
into a garden of graffiti.

But the puffy King
lived on, his painkillers
neutralizing, neutralizing,
until he became
ludicrous in performance.

The enthroned cannot revolt.
What was the pain
he needed to kill
if not the ultimate pain

of feeling no pain?

K A Y   M U R P H Y

Eighties Meditation

This picnic table's carefully etched
with faded JAGGER, DYLAN, ERIC CLAPTON,
HASH, COCAINE, DEEP PURPLE, PURPLE HAZE:
gods we prayed to in the late late Sixties.
That once charmed life flashes back, chips
of sun riding the water without touch,
to a weeping willow on the far bank
untouched by any god. It leans unknown
to itself over the water like a person
I never knew but used to love to be.

Fresher, deliberately deep, these three scars
sprawl over the others: FUCK THE WORLD.

Strangers: An Essay

Comment:
  "Tom Cruise should not play Jim."
Response:
  "He won't."
      —Graffiti, Père-Lachaise

Forget maps at 10F each. Those before
you left markers no birds carry off:
hundreds of *Jim*s with arrows in hot
pink fingernail polish on crypt
sides or street signs from any cemetery
entrance or intersection to his grave
—6th Division, east of Abélard and
Héloïse's, east of the Crematorium.

I got lost in the boulevard-and-avenue
lattice then found by a Frenchman
who crossed my path, glanced
back, mumbled, "Morrison?", crooked his
finger at my *mais oui,* and led me.

Three Dutch kids already there stood
silent as the slabs neighboring his, where
those before us scribbled,
    "Break on through to the other side,"
    "Come on, baby, light my fire,"
    "People are strange,"
to whom others answered,
    "Too drunk to fuck on this side,"
    "Jim, we want your babies,"

"Let Jim live. Stay strange."
—graffiti as much props in acts of
devotion or contrition as Chartres'
stained glass or its stone floor maze
through which penitents crawl on their
knees, crossing themselves.

Clairvoyants, the kids connect, however
they may, with the other side, scribbling
syllables meaning more to them and him
now than in two centuries, a dead
syntax musicologists or pop-culture freaks
will carbon date, translate, add as footnote
to treatises on an obsure Eastern
section of Paris or a shadowy American
prone to black leather and flashing
crowds, only more words gathering dust on
library shelves in world capitals.

The man who found me sweeps the grave
daily, collects cigarette butts and pint
whiskey bottles left by those who
leave something of themselves
behind, what nourishes and harms
simultaneously, what Morrison would've
recognized, understood, maybe even
blessed had he risen as our breath rose,
white and formless that chilly morning.

Then two more arrived, boys, Parisian,
one raven hair and raven eyes who sat
beside me, who—when the Calico
climbed into my lap, planted muddy paw
prints on my thighs, and jabbed his head
into my jacket arm pit—asked, "Know
his name?" then said, "Jim," when I shook
my head. He smiled at me, the stranger

here, the only one old enough to've watched
Morrison shake it at crowds, our peek
worth the ticket's cost, enough to keep
us horny and giggling for weeks.

   The boy began, "Come on, baby,
light. . . ." One by one the rest added
their voices, pronunciation perfect, cadence
misplaced, a tinny choir. Before he motioned
me to join in, I rose into wisps of
my breath, divined north by where the sun
perched in trees, and left to leave
stones for Edith Piaf and Paul Éluard.
No graffiti or hymns for them
—only flowers, plastic or wilting.

DOROTHY BARRESI

The Back-Up Singer

For C., for the original Coconuts

The father of the Stethoscope:
René Theophile Hyacinthe Laënnec,
mellifluous name.
In 1816 he rolled a *cornet de papier*, then held it
against the first chest
of the first heart to open its argument
to another man that way, through flesh
and conducting bone. Later
the instrument was crafted of wood, and a small hole bored
for the passage of human sound.

Is it wrong to want to be the only one?
To wish the wedding ring of the spotlight
slipped over me in a moment
that finally holds?
Houselights rise then lower like the rush of blood
through narrow vessels.
The cymbal solo and high hat
shimmer me forward, but in the blur
and slip of horns I'm singing *do wop*
and *shing, shing-a-ling*
behind a lame pimp and his big-haired girls.

I like to read the old school books.
The page of René Laënnec
turned down in particular, and nearly worn through,
which is also the nature of hope.

A young girl's hands turned
whole lifetimes down.

I'd listen to the telegraphing night bugs'
double ardor, and eventually to darkness
siphoned off by dawn
like the sounds I'd make with my perfect pitch
and years of training under that same blue
no-protection sky.

But there are planetary systems in the blood.
A grand opera of fate brings chances
we can't see but choose somehow.
Later, we see how we went wrong.
Now August says he never, ever
wanted anyone so badly. But there's rehab first,
and the business with his wife.
And the last abortion having left
a disability of my womb
I've come to think of as a million tiny birdsfeet tracking
over muddied ground. Some nights

it's too much like this
on the girls' bus. Regret or Spend It Now,
towels around our throats.
More often it's regret
rolling its bullet casings at our feet—
Lissanne, Yvette, me—
its spent and blackened flashbulbs.
Then I recall the lessons I never quite learned
for their sweetness alone.
On a single mating flight
the queen bee will store enough spermatozoa
to hold her the rest of her working days.
In the blue runways of iris and morning glory,
from ultraviolet
nectar guides, she'll fertilize as she goes.

Call it love that keeps me here.
Call it the final, female talent for demurring
when life takes over.
I call it a living, discovering at sixteen
that come in my mouth doesn't taste
remotely like white flowers.
Ten years later I'm waiting for the bus to stop
or lurch me to my next home.

I'm housewife to an act that pays and pays and pays.
Under lights hotter than God
I activate the angels in my voice and take
three steps backward, *cha cha cha.*
But I call it a science more mine
than either sex or shame
to be this alone, in time, among others.
Some days I get up before noon just to hear
the first notes of the treble world
break from my throat
over the heads of everyone listening but me.

LYNDA HULL

Midnight Reports

That's how billboards give up their promises—
they look right into your window, then whisper
sex, success. The Salem girl's smoke plume
marries the sky that reaches down to cut
deep gulfs between the high-rise projects,
the usual knife's-edge ballet enacted nightly there
for the benefit of no one. It's just that
around midnight every love I've known flicks open
like a switchblade and I have to start talking,
talking to drown out the man in the radio
who instructs me I'm on the edge of a new day
in this city of Newark which is not a city

of roses, just one big hock-shop. I can't tell you
how it labors with its grilled storefronts, air
rushing over the facts of diamonds, appliances,
the trick carnations. But you already know that.
The M-16 Vinnie sent—piece by piece—from Vietnam
is right where you left it the day you skipped town
with the usherette of the Paradise Triple-X Theater.
You like the way she played her flashlight down
those rows of men, plaster angels flanked around
that screen. Sometimes you'd go fire rounds over
the land fill, said it felt better than crystal meth,
a hit that leaves a trail of neon, ether.

I keep it clean, oiled, and some nights it seems
like a good idea to simply pick up that rifle

and hold it, because nothing's safe. You know how
it is: one minute you're dancing, the next you're flying
through plate glass and the whole damn town is burning
again with riots and looters, the bogus politicians.
We'd graduated that year, called the city ours,
a real bed of Garden State roses. I've drawn X's over
our eyes in the snapshot Vinnie took commencement
night, a line of X's over our linked hands. The quartet
onstage behind us sang a cappella—four brothers
from Springfield Ave. spinning in sequined tuxedos,

palms outstretched to the crowd, the Latin girls
from Ironbound shimmering in the brief conflagration
of their beauty, before the kids, before
the welfare motels, corridors of cries and exhalations.
You'd say all this was sentimental. But that night
I wore the heels you called my blue suede shoes,
and you'd given yourself a new tattoo, my name across
your bicep, in honor of finishing, in honor of the future
we were arrogant enough to think would turn out right.
I was laughing in that picture, laughing when the rain
caught us later and washed the blue dye from my shoes—
blue the color of bruises, of minor regrets.

DAVID KELLER

The Man Who Knew the Words to "Louie, Louie"

Impossible, the way one black walnut, fallen
from the tree at the top of the street rolled
some forty feet down the hill where in ten years
the tree across the street from my house grew,
and so on, slowly, slowly across the country
like a cousin who moved to Idaho you could stay with
if you were passing that way:
some place not completely unfamiliar.

At the theater, the movie'd been on half an hour,
so I bought an ice cream cone, disappointed,
and drove home slowly to the radio, summer
ending, the full moon only a week off.

They played "One Summer Night," from the 50's and "The Stroll"
by the Diamonds. I never knew it was their song;
I used to be crazy for them the year my family
was in Germany, a boys' school, and I felt far away. And then
"I Haven't Got Time for the Pain," Carly Simon,
and something by Elvis I knew too well to want to hear,
and "Louie Louie," and I thought how I never understood
the words.

The heat-lightning flickered like regret
against the trees and lawns, the years spent
living inside the music, afraid of being alone.
How little I've learned, the songs tell me.

I hate saying this, formal as the trees
or else with no better words than those songs,
the first language we learned to feel in.
The music's demeanor is unconsciously cheerful
as the adopted Vietnamese child's, with the tape
of songs and messages from the other orphans.
So she will not forget her old life.
Put away with the clothes she arrived in,

within weeks the tape speaks a language
less and less recognizable to her. Soon
she's learned English and no longer seems frightened.
How pleased her new parents are.

JAMES SEAY

"Johnny B. Goode"

What a wonderful dumb story of America: country boy
who never learned to read or write too well, but could play
a guitar just like ringing a bell and his mother
told him he would be a man, the leader
of a big old band, maybe someday his name in lights.
You couldn't count the times
Chuck Berry has duck-walked that song across the stage.
I'd say the draw is mostly rock and roll,
though I could probably write one of those pop-culture essays
on its All-American iconography,
the railroad running through the promise-land
and Johnny strumming to the rhythm the drivers made,
not to mention lost Eden
way back up in the woods among the evergreens.
We might hear all of that at some level,
I guess, and there must a kind of dramatic imperative
in his name we have to cheer for beyond rock and roll.
Sure, it's left tentative whether Johnny will see himself
in lights, but we know he's more than nominally good
and'll honor every tender dream his mother ever had.
It doesn't matter that the paradise of lights
is like any other paradise, a paradox down to its roots,
a walled-in park we die to get out of,
and that finally Johnny is going to be singing those songs
about wanting country roads to take him home,
back in time to the evergreens.
It doesn't matter because Johnny has got to get

into the Coupe de Ville just like Maybelline did,
the promise in every song they've ever heard.
And when we pull alongside in the V-8 Ford
we're barely going to be able to tell them apart
through the tinted glass: the one we're cheering for
and the one we're asking why can't she be true.

PETER BALAKIAN

Rock 'n Roll

The groove in black plastic got deeper

What was that light?

A migrant
I slid into a scat,

and in the purple silk
and the *Canoe*

there was sleekness and a rear-view mirror.

And the Angels flew out of the cloisonné vase
They were the rachitic forks hanging on the wall in the midnight
  kitchen.

And so I called you after the house was still.
My turquoise Zenith melting

And you asked: what was that light?

I was spinning. I was the trees shivering,
and the snake of coiled light on the ceiling
was moonglow.

I wasn't a fool in a satin tux.
I was Persian gold and teal blue.
I was the son of the Black Dog of Fate.

I said: I saw a rainbow of glass
above the Oritani Theater.

Lord, lead me from Hackensack New Jersey
into the white streak of exhaust.

Song of the Burning

I wanted the heart to scream.
I wanted the sound of chalk on a blackboard,
shrillness and pain
still echoing from childhood, another way

to talk around love.
I wanted it steady, pulsing of light
from a distant star, the Bo Diddley *thunk*
of drum and bass, the organ
crescendoing. *Who do you love? Who*
do you love? I wanted song without story,
only the cruelest metaphor. But who
finally gives a shit?
The body runs down.
Love turns to habit, and some nights you wail
or meth yourself past forgetting.
This is why you think some nights
you're Satan's poor facsimile, and why

you'll wake up dead one morning.
Talk around love: I mean that,
until love's all spell and incantation,
a name like GLORIA, and you sound
each letter out like need,
or show your cock to half the wasted
little punks of Miami, the strobes
all over you like hands.
In my dream, someone makes a movie

beginning with my song; first you see a jungle
resurrect to yellow flame, rise up
like outstretched arms. On
and on it burns until you'd think
the leaves themselves were howling.
This is the end, I'm singing,
beautiful friend, my only friend,
the flames want to wrap us
all in their hands, and that's
when I know what love is,
perfectly. Then maybe the band
gets projected on the screen, playing tighter
than they've ever been, and we've all
got those bleeding
flaming hearts of Mexican Christs.
We all understand where we're going.
And you all know, you poor dumb fuckers,

what you have to do to follow me.
It's the fifth of July, 1971, and I wake
in the best *pensione* in Paris. 4:00 a.m.
I start the day with speedball,
spoon a puddle of flame. Seven floors
below my window, a dwarf on crutches sells
the first edition of *Le Figaro*.

A couple walks arm in arm toward him,
a black guy, Algerian maybe,
the girl with straight blonde hair.
The black guy strokes
her ass as she buys the paper.
She points at something
in the air above them, as all the neon lights
in the city flicker off.

At hours like this you understand
there were songs you were never

able to write, Song Of The Burning,
Song Of Revelation, Song
That Is Past Forgetting.
At hours like this you rise
to address the ages, history,
the universe. You poor dumb bastards,

I swear you'll never hear my voice again.

ALEDA SHIRLEY

The Hours Musicians Keep

They were gestures out of a movie, I tell you;
before kissing me he took my wine glass
and placed it on the mantel with such care
it might have been a flame. With a tube
of 'Fire and Ice' he extended the seams
of my stockings up my spine.

                              You pour
two more fingers of bourbon. Opaque
with dawn, your eyes glint like metal
mirrors. You're lost in thought of Lonnie,
who with his sax filled bright rooms
with rain, modulated ambience and mood.
Maybe Lonnie was right, and repetition
is a kind of failure. Then why did he leave you
again and again? Now's as good a time
as any: I give you the combs given me
by the faithless flamenco guitarist. Touching

the ivory teeth I recall waking in his bed
as women sang from the rooftops of Seville.
Time is no cure; lately we've killed time,
you and I, with a polo player. Mad for us
both, he offers lizard handbags, private
beaches, lines of cocaine.

                         Is this the way
it would have been, Lynda, had we been born
four decades earlier? Sitting in a banquette,

requesting the band play "Satin Doll," would we
have found ordonnance in the improvised?
The torch singer's too lovely to bear.
Glamour can't conceal the attention detail
demands of her—the hundreds of sidemen
she knows by name, hours spent on phrasing.
And scat—the easiest thing in the world, she says;
I keep going because I refused to stop.

WILLIAM MATTHEWS

An Elegy for Bob Marley

In an elegy for a musician,
one talks a lot about music,
which is a way to think about time
instead of death or Marley,

and isn't poetry itself about time?
But death is about death and not time.
Surely the real fuel for elegy
is anger to be mortal.

No wonder Marley sang so often
of an ever-arriving future, that verb tense
invented by religion and political rage.
Soon come. Readiness is all,

and not enough. From the urinous
dust and sodden torpor
of Trenchtown, from the fruitpeels
and imprecations, from cunning,

from truculence, from the luck
to be alive, however, cruelly,
Marley made a brave music—
a rebel music, he called it,

though music calls us together,
however briefly—and a fortune.
One is supposed to praise the dead
in elegies for leaving us their songs,

though they had no choice; nor could

the dead bury the dead if we could pay
them to. This is something else we can't
control, another loss, which is, as someone

said in hope of consolation,
only temporary, though the same phrase
could be used of our lives and bodies
and all that we hope survives them.

CHRISTOPHER GILBERT

Time with Stevie Wonder in It

Winter, the empty air, outside
cold shaking its rigid tongue
announcing itself like something stone,
spit out, which is still a story
and a voice to be embraced.
Januaried movements but I hear a tune
carries me home to Lansing.

Always waiting for signs of thaw,
dark nomads getting covered by snow,
our parents would group in the long night—
tune frequencies to the Black stations
blasting out of Memphis, Nashville,
still playing what was played down south—
Ray Charles, Charles Brown, Ruth Brown, Muddy and Wolf.

The tribal families driven north
to neighborhoods stacked like boxes—
to work the auto plants was progress,
to pour steel would buy a car
to drive hope further on down the road.
How could you touch, hear
or be alive; how could anybody

wearing our habits, quiet Protestant
heads aimed up to some future?
This was our rule following—
buy at J. C. Penney and Woolworth's,
work at Diamond Reo, Oldsmobile, Fisher Body.

On Fridays drink, dance, and try to forget
the perverse comfort of huddling in

what was done to survive (the buffering,
the forgetting). How could we not
"turn the head/pretend not to see?"
This is what we saw: hope screwed
to steel flesh, this was machine city
and the wind through it—neutral
to an extent, private, and above all

perfectly European language
in which we could not touch, hear
or be alive. How could anybody
be singing "Fingertips"? Little Stevie
Wonder on my crystal, 1963.
Blind boy comes to go to school,
the air waves politely segregated.

If this were just a poem
there would be a timelessness—
the punchclock midwest would go on
ticking, the intervals between ticks
metaphor for the gap in our lives
and in that language which would not
carry itself beyond indifferent

consequences. The beauty of the word,
though, is the difference between language
and the telling made through use.
Dance Motown on his lip, he lays
these radio tracks across the synapse
of snow. The crystals show
a future happening with you in it.

SYDNEY LEA

The One White Face in the Place

So often true back then,
that platitude,
when in Harlem   Baltimore
north Philly   D.C.
I wasn't altogether
unwelcome in the blues
joints. I'd travel across
two states to see
the shuck-and-jive of Muddy
Waters' band,
the great Ray Charles, for whom
I'd travel farther,
the Lightnings (Slim and Hopkins),
Bobby Bland,
some wonderful unfamous
wreck named Arthur. . . .

Ray would cry out "Drown
in My Own Tears"
with that heartbreak keyboard tinkle
before the refrain.
Here in whitest New Hampshire
fifteen years
later, and seven states
away, the tin roof tinkles
with new rain
after a morning of purest
New England blue.

I walked the high-country beat,
for reminiscence. . . .
"*Every*body understands
them mean old blues!"
So Ray would shout. And then
as now, I sensed
that I might be included.
Right or wrong.

Today in the woods, the one
white face in the place,
I marveled that all that pain
could turn to song!
The testament of will. . . .
Just as out of their innards
the spiders' lace
had strung itself from every
bush and tree:
makings. And yet I thought,
high on the hill,
how—if indeed it's a fact
that on every acre there are
a million of these
deft spinners—then I was a million-
fold trailed and tracked,
attacked, fished for, observed,
climbed upon,
and caressed by design and brilliance.

What end do they serve?
One true fact is that
the one white
face in the place became
ever more overgrown
with the spiders' snares. I fought
through them as I fight
through many reminders. Reminders,

though, of what?
Well, maybe ambivalence if not
plain contradiction.
The webs are a sign of welcome
and malediction,
if spiders speak from their guts.
Yet, in another age,
these thready secretions
were regarded as stuff with which
to stanch a wound. . . .

It's as if what's ripped from us
becomes the thing that heals.
The blues: to understand them
is to be confounded.
Just so, walking such country,
Emerson feels
that "nothing is got for nothing."
I, the stranger,
understood—if I did—
the blues because
I *was* the stranger, at ease
because of the danger:
white boy in the dark
after the Blue Laws'
curfew amid the forbidden
tastes and odors
of gin, sweat, pomade
and Mary Jane.
And more overpowering than these
—hotter, harder—
that sense which comes again
with returning rain,
which blackens the world in order
to dress it in lightning
and drowns the fields in quiet

that they may speak
with the murmuring voice of a million
ancient waters;

that sense of a ray of hope
from out of the frightening
wreckage, and a thread of despair
from out of the bland
spun repetitions of handsome
brightblue days;
and from platitudinous matter
the makings of grand
structure, beauty, which are random
reminders still.

Dark blood pulses in the one
white face in the place
and will.

Decrescendo

If there is only one world, it is this one.

In my neighborhood, the ruby-helmeted woodpecker's line
Is all spondees, & totally formal as it tattoos
Its instinct & solitude into a high sycamore which keeps

Revising autumn until I will look out, &
Something final will be there: a branch in winter—not
Even a self-portrait. Just a thing.

Still, it is strange to live alone, to feel something
Rise up, out of the body, against all that is,
By law, falling & turning into the pointless beauty

Of calendars. Think of the one in the office closed
For forty-three summers in a novel by Faulkner, think
Of unlocking it, of ducking your head slightly
And going in. It is all pungent, & lost. Or

It is all like the doomed singers, Cooke & Redding,
Who raised their voices against the horns'
Implacable decrescendos, & knew exactly what they

Were doing, & what they were doing was dangerous.

The man on sax & the other on piano never had to argue
Their point, for their point was time itself; & all
That one wished to say, even to close friends,
One said beside that window: The trees turn; a woman
Passing on the street below turns up her collar against
The cold; &, if the music ends, the needle on the phonograph

Scrapes like someone raking leaves, briefly, across
a sidewalk, & no one alone is, particularly, special.

That is what musicians are for, to remind us of this, unless

Those singers die, one shot in a motel room
By a woman who made a mistake; & one dead
In a plane crash, an accident.

Which left a man on sax & another on piano
With no one to back up, &, hearing the news,
One sat with his horn in a basement in Palo Alto,
Letting its violence go all the way up, &
Annoying the neighbors until the police came,
And arrested him—who had, in fact, tears
In his eyes. And the other, a white studio
Musician from L.A., who went home & tried

To cleave the keyboard with his hands until
They bled, & his friends came, & called his wife,
And someone went out for bandages & more bourbon—

Hoping to fix up, a little, this world.

KEVIN STEIN

Upon Finding a Black Woman's Door Sprayed with Swastikas, I Tell Her This Story of Hands

How to say hate was in rancorous bloom,
    spiking my town's tepid April breath
with florets of white sheets & raised,
    gloved fists. How to say we seethed
around our school, white & black splayed

on either side of Lincoln Street, its broken
    promise. Tick, tick, tick, & I was late
for chemistry, prelude to explosion
    as flushed & spontaneous as any combustion
you'd swear won't happen, fists & chains

catalyzing our frothy breath. I screamed
    "Be cool, man!", beneath a pitiful catalpa,
beneath its blossoms the Creek called *kutuhlpa,*
    "head with wings," though some of us
had surely lost our head & any chance

of flight. I screamed "Peace!"
    & took a punch in my white face.
After the sirens & nightsticks, after
    snarling dogs & the mid-morning spritz
of Mace, after the curses & bloody lips,

we felt exotic, lured to some fine madness
    we'd never recover from. What I had
in mind involved my girlfriend, not Clayton

thumbing a ride, huge defensive end
who'd trashed halfbacks as he lilted

"Going to a Go-Go" and I piled on. His black
    hand swallowed mine, his knuckles bruised,
bleeding. We didn't say "brother." We didn't
    sing of slain Jack & Bobby & Martin.
We didn't swear we loved this life, either—

the woof & warp of hour upon hour tottering
    like a palace of the lost, beguiled,
befuddled. It wasn't exactly cruising,
    though we drove windows down, AM 1470
spooning out Smokey Robinson & the Miracles,

their honeyed voices as smooth as
    my parents' powder blue Bel-Air.
How to say I felt spring waft its redolent
    insistence across the cracked dash
& I harmonized with Bill "Smokey" Robinson.

How to say Clayton's hand daubed
    my split lip with iodine, all the while
a bloody sunset reeled in the night:
    fish of dark, fish of peace, speckled fish
of forgiveness he knew more of than I.

MICHAEL WATERS

Christ at the Apollo, 1962

For Andrew Hudgins

Even in religious fervor there is
a touch of animal heat.
—Walt Whitman

Despite the grisly wounds portrayed in prints,
the ropy prongs of blood stapling His eyes
or holes like burnt half-dollars in His feet,
the purple gash a coked teenybopper's
lipsticked mouth in His side, Christ's suffering
seemed less divine than the doubling-over
pain possessing "the hardest working man."
I still don't know whose wounds were worse: Christ's brow
thumb-tacked with thorns, humped crowns of feet spike-split—
or James Brown's shattered knees. It's blasphemy
to equate such ravers in their lonesome
afflictions, but when James collapsed on stage
and whispered *please please please,* I rocked with cold,
forsaken Jesus in Gethsemane
and, for the first time, grasped His agony.
Both rose, Christ in His unbleached muslin gown
to assume His rightful, heavenly throne,
James wrapped in his cape, pussy-pink satin,
to ecstatic whoops of fans in Harlem.
When resurrection tugs, I'd rather let
The Famous Flames clasp my hand to guide me
than proud Mary or angelic orders
still befuddled by unbridled passion.

Pale sisters foistered relics upon me,
charred splinter from that chatty thief's cross and
snipped thread from the shroud that xeroxed Christ's corpse,
so I can't help but fashion the future—
soul-struck pilgrims prostrate at the altar
that preserves our Godfather's three-inch heels
or, under glass, like St. Catherine's skull, *please*,
his wicked, marceled conk, his tortured knees.

BARON WORMSER

Soul Music

The Baltimore evening I saw
Otis and Aretha I knew
Kings and queens existed after all:
Something good and true and danceable,
The uncharted earthbound hit.

They said to believe and leap.
The nation no longer was diagrammatic;
Unsevered feeling fit
Into anybody's skin.
Unthwarted sound was the test
Of embodied, unchurched progress.

Outside that night
Plate glass fractured like
A sobbing final tone,
A plea which brought white men
To the city on a Sunday afternoon
To watch the condemned frolic
At everyone's expense.

Whole blocks burned gladly,
The stuff of democratic
Promise freely redeemed,
The grandeur of performance
Burlesqued by riot.

I, too, protested:
Hadn't I been good,

Hadn't I endorsed
Both sympathy and force?
Didn't I love the music
As much as I could?

On the televised streets
I saw people dancing,
Souls on fire with a passion
That sang of days
No ticket could touch.

MARK JARMAN

The Supremes

In Ball's Market after surfing till noon,
we stand in wet trunks, shivering
as icing dissolves off our sweet rolls
inside the heat-blued counter oven,
when they appear on his portable TV,
riding a float of chiffon as frothy
as the peeling curl of a wave.
The parade m.c. talks up their hits
and their new houses outside of Detroit
and old Ball clicks his tongue.
Gloved up to their elbows, their hands raised
toward us palm out, they sing,
"Stop! In the Name of Love" and don't stop
but slip into the lower foreground.

Every day of a summer can turn,
from one moment, into a single day.
I saw Diana Ross in her first film
play a brief scene by the Pacific—
and that was the summer it brought back.
Mornings we paddled out, the waves
would be little more than embellishments:
lathwork and spun glass,
gray-green with cold, but flawless.
When the sun burned through the light fog,
they would warm and swell,
wind-scaled and ragged,
and radios up and down the beach

would burst on with her voice.

She must remember that summer
somewhat differently, and so must the two
who sang with her in long matching gowns,
standing a step back on her left and right,
as the camera tracked them
into our eyes in Ball's Market.
But what could we know, tanned white boys,
wiping sugar and salt from our mouths
and leaning forward to feel their song?
Not much, except to feel it
ravel us up like a wave
in the silk of white water,
simply, sweetly, repeatedly,
and just as quickly let go.

We didn't stop either, which is how
we vanished, too, parting like spray—
Ball's Market, my friends and I.
Dredgers ruined the waves,
those continuous dawn perfections,
and Ball sold high to the high rises
cresting over them. His flight out of L.A.,
heading for Vegas, would have banked
above the wavering lines of surf.
He may have seen them. I have,
leaving again for points north and east,
glancing down as the plane turns.
From that height they still look frail and frozen,
full of simple sweetness and repetition.

YUSEF KOMUNYAKAA

Tu Do Street

Music divides the evening.
I close my eyes & can see
men drawing lines in the dust.
America pushes through the membrane
of mist & smoke, & I'm a small boy
again in Bogalusa. *White Only*
signs & Hank Snow. But tonight
I walk into a place where bar girls
fade like tropical birds. When
I order a beer, the mama-san
behind the counter acts as if she
can't understand, while her eyes
skirt each white face, as Hank Williams
calls from the psychedelic jukebox.
We have played Judas where
only machine-gun fire brings us
together. Down the street
black GIs hold to their turf also.
An off-limits sign pulls me
deeper into alleys, as I look
for a softness behind these voices
wounded by their beauty & war.
Back in the bush at Dak To
& Khe Sanh, we fought
the brothers of these women
we now run to hold in our arms.
There's more than a nation

inside us, as black & white
soldiers touch the same lovers
minutes apart, tasting
each other's breath,
without knowing these rooms
run into each other like tunnels
leading to the underworld.

JIM POWELL

It Was Fever That Made the World

It was fever that made the world
burn last summer, that afternoon
when I lay watching the sun pour
its incurable folly slantwise
into a plum tree's crest,

infusing it till the whole crown glowed
red as infected blood translucent
in a syringe. Sunlight was
the carnal fuel leaves burned for life—
obedient to hunger,

they turned their faces toward it
with such greed, in their recklessness
I could see fall's wreckage breeding:
motionless, each leaf swarmed
with an earthly fire

commanding as the power I felt
churning inside me last night
listening to a guitar rant
dirty blues till the crowd eddied
open as everyone

started dancing: past will
or withstanding, in the hot dark
song after song grew stronger, thriving
like summer in our shaken limbs.
Outside, between sets,

after midnight in the sidewalk
company of strangers, all
the flushed faces reminded me:
sweat was a fever sign last June—now,
my drenched shirt cooling

felt like health, like strength, urgent as the sight
of taillights queuing at the tollbooths
Friday night, then streaming up the bridge
till all five lanes of their sharp reds merge
toward the city's bright towers.

Dirty blues courtesy of Garcia

DAVID RIVARD

Consolation

For Dianne

There is none. And this means today,
Saturday, I have a reason to walk 24th Street.
Chromed lowrides jam by for *chicas*.
And if you needed reasons this badly
you'd linger too, watching an early sixties
white Chevy convertible, streaming cool brilliance,
as it trails a nineteen-year-old sales clerk who swished out
the Tico House of Beauty. Silver crucifix earrings,
razor-cut hair, magenta lipstick. And over Prince funking
from the radio's blast, when they call to her, *Valerie,*
I swear, it almost might sound to you like, *Hey,*
pal of the dream! But I've lived eight months
in this district, lots of jittery eyes, laughing,
kids wailing at bus stops. No rapture. Scraps
of newsprint, kleenex, candy wrappers snap
across the intersection. Strange that a wind this strong
makes shoppers seem strong trudging into it.
Someone stops to ask me a question in Spanish,
near the library, & I can't answer. Near somebody
bundled in fake mink, wool scarf,
shivering in eighty-degree heat, brown hand scribbling
furiously across greasy, ruled notepaper,
erasing the minutes. Never mind what fury it is
that drives the pen, I can't tell if it's a woman or man.
Why shouldn't I admit I don't understand? Not the question,
not the cold body bent over, or anyone else's

indecipherable life.
                              Each day, brackish & shining,
the bay swings twice to the ocean, twice back.
Every night at dusk the hillsides of condos & homes flicker on
above Castro. Enough for me to think, sure, those lights
will go on every day. Until my next thought
shuts them off, a scratch on crumpled paper
that reports some days everything stops. The day
my friend lost her baby,
can't be undone, or held down. I'd been writing her a letter,
her small body tearing itself up. And that pain
I couldn't think what to say. Went out,
the morning hot, windy. There's a slick guy
stuck at a traffic light, gunning his engine.
I have to listen—like a heartbeat after an accident,
racing, racing.

CHARLES BAXTER

The Purest Rage

This thing happens in mid-summer,
and at an intersection under a washed-out sky
lit as usual by the chafing sun,
and we're all lined up at one red light.
We're being dutiful, and it's July,
as if the gods told God it would have to be like this,
and then they died, and it still is.
I'm on my way to fill the lawn mower's can
with antique, lethal, leaded gasoline.

All these cars have their drivers' windows down,
and it's a battle of the bands; Van
Halen over here, and (I think) Sting,
cacophony pleasing to the ear, but then
I notice on my left this Riviera, a living room
on wheels, windows closed to keep the cool air in.
I look over: *he* and *she,*
both oddly young, and she, not driving,
is shouting patiently, her eyes fixed straight ahead.
I read her lips. The only word I see is "Yes."

Still the background of the music,
and her silent shouting whose pure rage
makes her neck cords stand out visibly and tight,
and I think, *she's my age.* I glance
at the man behind the wheel, absorbing this,
glasses, slicked hair, white shirt, blue silk tie.
And then they're gone, and I'm being honked at,

and I accelerate, wanting to see just one last time
the full hopelessness of their errand
to push her anger against his blank stare.
But I don't catch them. They're not there.

But I think of the afternoon (you told me)
you saw the back yard's maple in a storm
and whipped by winds that summer of bad weather.
You thought: *I shouldn't see this, I should be downstairs,*
but as you watched you thought the tree
was in a rage because it looked like it,
and there were no words to make it less.
Whipped by the wind on its way somewhere,
and though you knew, you said, it was a fallacy,
the tree was enraged because it stayed
right there, obedient, rooted, crazed
by simple loyalty to the ground it grew in.

CHRISTOPHER GILBERT

Chosen to Be Water

Across the field the great willow rocking its head
back and forth in the waters of the wind
might mean a hard storm, but who notices?
Suddenly the rain against the westward windows
arrives hard, but honest enough to dictate
the season. Bob Marley is dead today, and
the woman's neighbor aims the bass in his stereo
to match the raindrops' episodic flaring—
but not the dark explosions where they strike
the glass, and not the lament this acid will
etch into the garden which collects it.
She imagines a cabbage out there,
wet, standing out against the moist black ground
like a pimple glistening or else a teardrop.
A leaf breaks from it, joining the spill
washed down between rows, and she says, *teardrop.*
Right now the chip on her shoulder is so sharp
she has no need to be disinterested
in pursuing the simile further, as the leaf
flows slowly downhill towards a gully.
She says the fallen leaf is a tear, too.
Suddenly she swears and shakes a sweat off—
squeezes her hips hard while she hums a song.
She wants the bold stroke of intense change.
Music has chosen her to be water again.
Is it raining in her neighbor's apartment?
She will go see, and pushes herself up
from a table already wet with her judgement.

FRANK O'HARA

The Day Lady Died

It is 12:20 in New York a Friday
three days after Bastille day, yes
it is 1959 and I go get a shoeshine
because I will get off the 4:19 in Easthampton
at 7:15 and then go straight to dinner
and I don't know the people who will feed me

I walk up the muggy street beginning to sun
and have a hamburger and a malted and buy
an ugly NEW WORLD WRITING to see what the poets
in Ghana are doing these days
                                  I go on to the bank
and Miss Stillwagon (first name Linda I once heard)
doesn't even look up my balance for once in her life
and in the GOLDEN GRIFFIN I get a little Verlaine
for Patsy with drawings by Bonnard although I do
think of Hesiod, trans. Richmond Lattimore or
Brendan Behan's new play of *Le Balcon* or *Les Nègres*
of Genet, but I don't, I stick with Verlaine
after practically going to sleep with quandariness

and for Mike I just stroll into the PARK LANE
Liquor Store and ask for a bottle of Strega and
then I go back where I came from to 6th Avenue
and the tobacconist in the Ziegfeld Theatre and
casually ask for a carton of Gauloises and a carton
of Picayunes, and a NEW YORK POST with her face on it

and I am sweating a lot by now and thinking of
leaning on the john door in the 5 SPOT
while she whispered a song along the keyboard
to Mal Waldron and everyone and I stopped breathing

DENIS JOHNSON

Heat

Here in the electric dusk your naked lover
tips the glass high and the ice cubes fall against her teeth.
It's beautiful Susan, her hair sticky with gin,
Our Lady of Wet Glass-Rings on the Album Cover,
streaming with hatred in the heat
as the record falls and the snake-band chords begin
to break like terrible news from the Rolling Stones,
and such a last light—full of spheres and zones.
August,
                you're just an erotic hallucination,
just so much feverishly produced kazoo music,
are you serious?—this large oven impersonating night,
this exhaustion mutilated to resemble passion,
the bogus moon of tenderness and magic
you hold out to each prisoner like a cup of light?

MICHAEL WATERS

American Bandstand

The boy rehearsing the Continental Stroll
before the mirror in his bedroom—
does he memorize the sweep of hair
tumbling across his eyes
when he spins once, then claps his hands?

Home from school in winter,
he studies the couples on television,
their melancholy largo,
how they glide together, then separate.
Such dancing makes him nervous—
so many hand motions to remember,
where to slide his feet, and
every girl in the gym staring at him.

That boy was familiar, twenty years ago,
saying hello to a loneliness
peculiar to the tender, the high-strung
lanterns suspended above the dance floor,
ousting shadows, leaving him
more alone, trapped in the spotlight.

The Peppermint Twist, The Bristol Stomp,
The Hully Gully are only memory,
but loneliness still dances
among the anxious ghosts of the heart,
preparing to stroll

down a line formed by teenagers
mouthing lyrics, clapping hands,
forever awkward,
each partner dreaming of grace.

RITA DOVE

"Hully Gully"

Locked in bathrooms for hours,
daydreaming in kitchens
as they leaned their elbows
into the shells of lemons,

they were humming, they were humming
Hully Gully. Summer lasted

a long time; porch geraniums
rocked the grandmothers to sleep
as night slugged in, moon riding the sky
like a drop of oil on water. Then down
the swollen pitch of avenue
discourteous blouses, bright rifflings,
gum popping to an invisible beat,

daughters floating above the ranks of bobby socks.
Theirs was a field to lie down in
while fathers worked swing shift and
wives straightened oval photographs
above the exhausted chenille
in bedrooms upstairs everywhere. . . .

MARK DEFOE

"Dream Lover"

Dream lover, where are you
with a love so fair and true?
—Bobby Darrin

Once they stood tiptoe, dewy, poised
before going down, going all the way,
parting with that pearl of wisdom
passed down by mom, mom who stood proud
before her new dishwasher and whispered
"Don't give yourself away. Bargain for it."

In dreams they tumble for me fresh,
yet middle-aged in lechery,
erotic from nostalgic angles
in multiples of two. And how they squeal,
spurring me on, me the stallion ghost
of Fabian, Elvis, and Troy Donahue.

I thumb the yearbook. I know now
how to flip on a certain charm.
Then those royalty didn't know I breathed.
Those queens with Mona Lisa smiles
as bland as folded razors,
can still leap out to bleed my foolish heart.

But where are you who got stuck with me?
I, bench rider, splinter-collector.
You who cartwheeled almost high enough
for cheerleader. Weren't we a number once?
You, filling out your fuzzy sweater.

Me, dudded out in letter jacket.

Remember when our lips made every song
a rhapsody of cuddly teenage truth?
Remember when we groped for paradise
in the backseat at the passion pit?

Fallen angel, though some enchanted evening
we would never know each other across
a crowded room, have we misplaced
the address to our hearts? Didn't we
go steady for almost six months?
Didn't you allow my ring to sway
in the sacred valley between your breasts?

Call me, call me collect across the years.
The yearbook's wrong. I'm sure that one perfect dance,
in your perfect dress, after my perfect game,
we were elected king and queen of something.

WILLIAM MATTHEWS

The Penalty for Bigamy Is Two Wives

I don't understand how Janis Joplin did it, how she made her voice break out like that in hives of feeling. I have a friend who writes poems who says he really wants to be a rock star—the high-heeled boots, the hand-held mike, the glare of underpants in the front row, the whole package. He says he likes the way music throws you back into your body, like organic food or heroin. But when he sings it is sleek and abstract except for the pain, like the silhouette of a dog baying at the moon, almost liver-shaped, a bell hung from a rope of its own pure yearning. Naturally his life is exciting, but sometimes I think he can't tell the difference between salvation and death. When I listen to my Janis Joplin records I think of him. Once I got drunk & sloppy and told him I feared artists always had more fun and more death, too, and how I had these strong feelings but nothing to do with them and he said *Don't worry I'd trade my onion collection for a good cry, wouldn't you?* I didn't really understand but poetry is how you feel so I lie back and listen to Janis's dead voice run up and down my body like a fire that has learned to live on itself and I think *Here it comes, Grief's beautiful blow job.* I think about the painter who was said to paint with his penis and I imagine one of his portraits letting down a local rain of hair around his penis now too stiff to paint with, as if her diligent silence meant to say *You loved me enough to make me, when will I see you next?* Janis, I don't care what anybody thinks or writes, I don't care if my friend who writes poems is a beautiful fake, like a planetarium ceiling, I want to hold my life in my arms as easily as my body will hold forever the silence for which the mouth slowly opens.

RONALD WALLACE

Sound Systems

Christmas, 1957. The Dell-Vikings and the Diamonds
playing the neural patterns in my brain
that will recall this place and time
over thirty years later, there in that hapless future
of Dolby, Walkman, Boom Box, and Disk
where everything has always already happened.

I am twelve, thinking of Nancy Bowers and of how
we'll sit in my basement rec room, necking
to "Little Darlin'," "Love Me Tender," "Honeycomb,"
as my father from his wheelchair in his study
calls out to keep it down, and Buddy Holly,
The Big Bopper, and Richie Valens leave the ground.

And then the music's over,
the old turntable rasping, around and around.

DAVID RIVARD

Cures

The part of the soul that doubts, again and again,
is scratchy as this song, "Mystery Train," where Elvis
relates some dark to himself. Even the light
in the living room seems sullen. We've turned the stereo
up loud, don't have to talk. After the latest argument,
trading blame is all that is left. After all that,
forgiveness? More punishment? Forgetting?
You curl, knees up, on the couch. Along your bare neck
the skin looks soft—shadows, the barrage
of falling brown hair, soft. I'm in the raggedy armchair,
and the music just washes through those questions,
then pours out the screen door. So this is what we do,
how we feel, each doubt a little larger
than desire, so that nothing
seems enough. And for a while,
ten minutes, I've stared at the album cover.
The face with the half-sneered, boyishly charming smile
stares back from the floor. The words echo wall to wall,
then silence as one song ends and we wait for the next.
What do we think? His smoothness and raveling wail will cure us
of all this? These rockabilly blues
from the early Memphis days, a shy country kid
opening for Pee Wee Crayton at the Flamingo Club.
When all he cared about was shouting the next tune.

The next tune. But endings are truer
for all their need: a mansion outside town,
years of Seconal, gaudy stage suits. Ways to simplify

the hundred confusions screaming in the body,
to become a star, or something stranger. . . .
I'd like to go over and brush away the hair
from your face. All the questions,
all the night, as it strikes
the house like a train whistle. And after I get up,
cross the room, you and I aren't sorry
it leads to this kiss. Or to what it brings on,
a soothing that lasts only so long,
like stardom
in America, or now this silence between songs.

ROCHELLE NAMEROFF

Elvis Presley

I want to get the screams in here—
the ones we danced to, shook to, laughed at,
hoping they'd never stop.
Screams we knew nothing about really
as we watched him jiggle and sneer,
his legs like electric rubber bands
which snapped so gorgeously in those zones
we were forbidden to claim. *Zones*
were for parking, and we understood that,

our bodies carefully sectioned into spots:
above the neck (was that why it was called
"necking"?) and *below,* like heaven and hell.
It's both, isn't it, and as we watched
that earthquake on the Magnavox,
our mouths knew something was happening
with unstopped noises all the way through.
How many saints applauded in our tongues?
How many victorian souls?

Our parents stuck out their thick hands too—
over their ears, over our eyes, all over
the press, their fingers shaking NO in the air,
as we shook free of their world, the new
holy rollers, and they knew it.

ROBERT WRIGLEY

The Prophecy

The minister's enunciations cut like knives.
He laid his great hand, pale and freckled,
on my shoulder, and made his prophecy.
I stood in my tie and white choir robe
and blushed. The truth was not so much
that I didn't love rock and roll,
but that I loved even more my father's jazz,
songs full of smoke and whiskey, ache and want.
Someday, he said, I would be a preacher,
and my parents behind me grinned, nervous
with the lie we'd not quite told.

The truth is, I didn't give a damn
what we sang, as long as we were singing.
We wondered why the rest of it
couldn't be abandoned: the crazed
responsive readings printed in the programs,
the rot of sermons and their barely veiled threats,
that hell we knew early on
we'd likely never avoid. Soprano boys,
we kept our voices one last year
above the cracks, three of us
in the sacristy drinking communion wine
with Debra, giggling and large-breasted
and lonely. Button by button, hook
by hook, she slowly slipped the robe
from her shoulders, opened her blouse
and lifted the loosened bra from her breasts.

No papery wafer tasted so rich
with salvation, no catechism felt so true.
And Sundays thereafter we sang
with the conviction of saints and met each week
in the sacristy for the confirmation of our flesh.

Still, the truth is a blade and cuts.
We feared the minister, though he owned a dozen suits.
Debra kissed us and laughed. In that room
we couldn't have sung for anything,
not for heaven, not for the hell of fear or betrayal,
not for one last touch the day Debra
declined to bare herself to us,
but only drank, sip and sip, all of us grown
quiet in the glowering, half-holy light.
By Easter our voices were ragged with baritone,
we'd given ourselves over to dancing and drums,
the searing violence of electric guitars,
behind which we wailed and sang.

PAUL MARIANI

Betty

And the fumbling. Oh blesséd Lord the fumbling,
the sweetness of that fumbling, when the Code,
the massive etched-in-adamantine moral Code,
self-imposed with spit-polished discipline,
at last began breaking into jagged ice-floe
pieces, as with that bronze imposing too huge
statue of Josef Stalin roped round
& pulled crumpling down on the cobbled streets
of Budapest as I myself had seen the fall before
on the twelve-inch black & white in the refectory
there at Beacon, and heard the whole thing
come crashing down my aching heavy cortex
against the still warm transmission hump rising
from beneath the cramped back seat of Grippie's
fifty-something Ford, where I sat erect
half kneeling at attention
before the plush dark brilliance that was Betty
breathing gardenia-scented-soft before me.

The frayed, parched edge of summer & the fall,
the long-awaited monsoon of the fall:
September, dark & warm, Saturday evening
easing into the equal darkness
of an early Sunday morning, the haloed cicada
glow of a single humming streetlight
with its scalloped-edged reflector
& the waft of music as it lifted into the warm
"Goodnight Sweetheart, well, I really must go,

goodnight sweeeeeet heart, goodnight,"
those black billowing cathedral-high arched elms
awash with the benediction of the present.

That year, that now-done year at Beacon Prep
with its benzine-bright Sublime, those moiling
waters as at Niagara Falls suspended at the edge
in a momentary semblance of transcendence
even as they fell, kept forever falling, as Grippie
and my brother & the others somehow seemed to know,
which was why of all the streets in Mineola
I think we'd finally parked just two streets down
from the local Catholic high school
where all the heroic bifurcated tension had begun.

I can still hear the mocking easy words
of Grippie, busy negotiating the unyielding
steering wheel & the five feet of the Ford's
front seat, that readymade divan & his sweetheart
on it with the six feet of his frame. "Hey, priest,"
he quips, "ain't this better than the stuff
they fed you at the Sem? Fer chrissake kiss her
& stop yer halfassed agonizing for a minute."

But by now even I need no antiphonary prompting
for such heart-pounding adoration
as my fingers touch in trembling disbelief
the throbbing vein along her neck, the flush
of yellowpurple silken skin, those plumdark lips
uplifted towards me, as bells, bells,
the silver tinkling tintinabulation of the bells
begin ringing as at the Easter celebration
somewhere deep within my head, sweeter even
than the angelus we sang in May by candlelight
before the phallocentric garden statue
of Our Lady when fifty boys crooned
their blesséd Aves deep into the mothblown

scented night, such lovely trembling,
curve of breast & swelling boss of nipple
reforming just beneath her thin white sweater,
which I vowed there & then ever to defend
from harm or other violation, even
as I sank my head into the space between her neck
and shoulder, praising Him for all the good
I'd found here in the midst of so much darkness . . .
as in that other garden, when clay first formed
& then awoke amazed to taste the first fruits
of that strange & lovely complementary shape
& I came off my earnest, stringent year-long fast
& kissed her lips & dear God tasted woman once again.

RICHARD FOERSTER

Playland

The 8-track clicked through tunes as we two
cruised from heady Bronxville down to Rye
in my '66 eggshell blue
Volkswagen. Jesuit-schooled, I tried

to be all a Catholic girl would want:
left hand suavely at the wheel; right hand
on her knee; plus bon-vivant
banter and *The Lonely Hearts Club Band*.

We joined the paired and wholesome troops
beneath the razzled night
and shrieked through Cyclone loop-the-loops,
then braved the hokey House of Frights,

but when my student's budget failed
we walked the dark along the shore.
There the steady obligato of the male
swelled above the fun park's roar.

We sat by rocks and listened to the Sound's
clouded water lap, then clamber
and withdraw. I cupped her breast, wound
a finger through her hair. My tongue remembered

silent speech, but soon she pushed
my lips away and pointed with surprise:
Everywhere were phosphorescent fish,
a thousand up-turned saintly eyes.

PAUL MCRAY

Performance

For Tom Patton, who was there

She came to this local bar,
soaring on some kind of speed or dust,
a gift for the men downing
their shots and drafts.
A quarter in the box hired the Jefferson Airplane
for ten minutes or so, and she danced
like nothing else mattered.
I've seen better than that,
a voice urged, *I've seen better.*
So she disappeared

into the women's room, hollering,
When I tell you, play D-22.

D-22, she called out,
and on the first note of "Dance with Me,"
she exploded into the dullness,
a xenon angel to a dozen men,
a bearer of simple grace,
an artist in the only way she could figure out
on a warm afternoon in 1972.
She wore just red socks and tennis shoes,
and her feet hardly touched the floor
as she spun her terror,

transfigured in the moment.
I still remembered how we never once saw

the eyes in this face,
and on this first cold night
in the fall of 1986
I can't remember the name
of that girl:
Randi, it might have been,
and there's no need
to ask how or why, or whether anyone
had kissed her lilting, sinking life even once,
and meant it.

JUDITH BERKE

Dancing to the Track Singers
at the Nightclub

A plastic freezer bag filled with cocaine, worn
as a cape, slung over the back
of the woman in the 50's black cinch-waist dress
and the 40's flowered and veiled
hat. So much is real then. If the past
is real. Or remembered.
The song is a hit, but what matters
is that the 3 young women move their lips
in exact sync with the tape—
the electronic drums, electric
guitars. The reverbs. The voices
laid in perfectly over that. Originally
it was Gloria, June and Grace
but then Grace left, so they had to get another
brunette. Someone's back in the john
using his own plastic bag to buy
a few lines from the larger
plastic container. Here in the club
the dancers are beginning to get their belongings
together. Mostly high school kids.
Big wide hair. Studs on their belts. Loafers.
The club is nearly empty
except for the 3 singers, who begin to sing
an old Stevie Wonder number.
No tape, so they sing it a cappella,
their eyes closed, winging it,

the way you'd sing
if there were nothing to sing but birds,
or maybe a few strings
and a bass: what's there, and what isn't
there, in the music.

DOROTHY BARRESI

Nine of Clubs, Cleveland, Ohio

Thursday night: Progressive
Friday and Saturday nights: Eurostyle

Now I know there are bored, beautiful people everywhere.
The boys on their long stems of bones
waft and mingle, sipping Campari,

saying next to nothing to the girls.
Ecstasy is draining.
So is awe, anger, dread, tenderness

when frustrated by convention—any number of emotions
we will not see here tonight,
though we stand equidistant from dancefloor

and Lake Erie, gone back to solution this March
the way a bruise leaves a body.
All night ice loosens and grinds toward Canada.

We feel it more than hear,
and ore boats steer darkly
into the issuance of their lights, their names, as we did

not one hour ago, supplicants in the doorway's
jittery neon. We paid eight dollars to enter
what is spare, cool, clean.

We left behind fish stink and diesel fuel.
But what Europe is this?
Like the music, the dancers' faces

would give no clues. They are whiter than pain

or distraction; their arms dovetail as though
beneath black turtlenecks

a cavity waited, red and humming, for larval wings
to fold twice, re-enter.
I think this is the end of immigration.

I think if a live pig were thrown
skating and shitting onto the gorgeous dancefloor,
no one would stop posing, or crouch down,

knife between his teeth
and stroking the smooth parquet croon
hunger, hunger, hunger

in his blood's first language.
The suburbs have given back their angels.
Refineries rise then sink like wedding cakes

into the filthy river—we've seen it often enough—
and it is wrongheaded or lachrymose
to wish the Old World back as well,

with its babushkas and lamentations, prayer cloths,
boats reeking of garlic cloves
by which we washed up on these shores. And the scythe

whistling at its uppermost arc—
"Di Provenza il mar, il suol."
The shining field,

the ugly babies in the architecture
puffing their thousand-year cheeks at us: I think
it wasn't ours, the past, and now

will never be, who left for better footing,
this purchase on brighter, quicker ground.
No tourist is ever innocent.

Tonight the music churns from hip to hip. The strobe light
won't make up its mind, but flickering hi-speed

erases half of all we see.

It's almost fun, this dancing.
And after, if the foreheads of the warehouses loom down
like character actors whose names

we're forever forgetting, say Ma Joad
or the Little Rascal's truant officer, that's okay.
We're lucky. Our car is right where we left it.

We're tired, sure. A little drunk.
The windshield weeps in a circle of streetlamp light and fog,
but we can drive all night if we want,

lose the lake lolling between these buildings
like a coated tongue,
head south to Akron or Columbus, or Xenia,

anywhere people routinely rise
from the abscence of themselves, and begin the day new.
As we will here tonight in the tiny

bathroom crowded with our tribe and generation
bowing to mirrors,
the glimpse of smokey, downturned faces—
you, me, in ritual greeting to our neatly razored lines.

LISEL MUELLER

The Deaf Dancing to Rock

The eardrums of the deaf are already broken; they like it loud. They dance away the pain of silence, of a world where people laugh and wince and smirk and burst into tears over words they don't understand. As they dance the world reaches out to them, from the floor, from the vibrating walls. Now they hear the ongoing drone of a star in its nearly endless fall through space; they hear seedlings break through the crust of the earth in split-second thumps, and in another part of the world, the thud of billions of leaves hitting the ground, apart and together, in the intricate rhythmic patterns we cannot hear. Their feet, knees, hips, enact the rhythms of the universe. Their waving arms signal the sea and pull its great waves ashore.

JIM ELLEDGE

"Their Hats Is Always White"

Just an hour before the hump of last night, when—not with an old-fashioned ringing but high-tech, high-pitched trills—the phone slit ear to ear the throat of his latest, best dream (How easily dinosaurs—big ones!—plopped to their knees when his whizzing club plunked against their heads. How light the woman's body—a big one!—grew, her hair coiling up his wrist.), he leapt up out of bed, untangling from lasso blankets, more naked than breath #1 to answer a dial tone.

Oops! Not his. The lady's next door. Their common wall a bulletin board of cigarette hacking, coo-coo clock chirps, bedspring wheezes.

Like a radio shrink on the graveyard shift reciting parables in kilowatts until cock-crow, her voice clawed at plaster, drawing blood.

"I saw Elvis today," she said. She said, "At the Washing Well." "Pulled up in a black, stretch Caddy spit-shined," she said. She said, "White jump suits tumble-drying in the cutest little tango." "He said Vegas was A-OK and tell ever'body he luvs 'em, specially them stayed fans through thick an' thin," said. Said, "Just needed a vacation. That's all." "Wrote 'To Lola from The King' in magic marker on them happy-face bikinis Ronny Lee gave me last Valentine's Day," said. Said, "I was tossin' no-static strips into dryers, and *woosh,* he vanished in thin air." "Thought I'd died and gone to my reward," she said.

Light filled the tabby's water dish and the kitchen sink, dusted the dining room table and TV cable box, fell onto the Persian carpet in game-board squares.

Outside, a flying saucer hovered about to land. A blink later, no: a full moon rounded through clouds that got clean away.

S U S A N   S W A R T W O U T

I Wannabe Your Queen

Give hugs, not drugs.

Elvis, King of PTL TV,
Hear my prayer of sincerity.

Sans Vous, I wander (lonely cloud)
Or crank the radio so loud

My pelvis feels the slammed reception.
Is it Immaculate Conception?

O Elvis, send your golden rain,
Ease my dark and stormy pain.

If I could bear your spirit child,
I'd rake in royalties like wild.

Of course, that's not my first concern.
In Country Hell, I'd rather burn

Than profit from your Heavenly Power,
But it's more certain than the hour

Each Saturday when they grab their balls
On TV for the lotto-calls.

I'd rather grab yours, Elvis dear,
Believing in your Message Clear

That everybody (*shake*) must rock.
And knowing my internal clock

Gives me just five more years to bake
In my oven an Elvis cake—

A son to be my Teddy Bear—
Surely, King, you are aware

That you could do a lot for me,
Maybe in *Time*, perhaps TV.

I go now to your sacred bower
In Memphis where the dogwoods flower,

Hoping you'll deflower me
Whilst I pace Thy cemetery

Without any underwear.
So if You love me, if You care,

Take me, Elvis, make me Queen
Of *I Saw Elvis* magazine.

VAN K. BROCK

Mary's Dream

I was living in New York.
He was dancing on the skyline.
I dreamed he was playing his guitar.
I couldn't believe he was dead.
He was made of iron welded to the stars
but danced in the air like flames.
The city blurred. It was part of him
waving at me. Then it was me.
That's when I knew he would never die.
He would always be the king. Look!
I'm too heavy and not pretty, but we
were one. One hand on my neck
squeezed tight, gently, as he held me,
his separate fingers moving all over
my body like musical notes on the sheet.
I was a cloud filled with colored lights,
but as lightning, when it strikes,
moves everywhere, everywhere it touched
sprouted flames. I was the music.
My whole body. It came from his mouth
and out of me, every pore, every wisp
of angel hair shivering and singing,
and it was then he called me by my name.
"Mary, I want you to go to Graceland.
It'll mean a lot to me."
So I came.

BARON WORMSER

Fans

When Janis Joplin died,
Some people silently applauded, saying
That it went to show you can't fool around,
That she had it coming,
A bad woman, dope fiend
And that sort of world-gone-to-hell thing.
I went out back of the house and cried
Till I was spent from crying.
I lay on the October ground

But felt no peace
        and felt I never would gain peace
In this world of pursy fatalists.
My friend Raymond insisted
That white people shouldn't mix with the blues,
They couldn't handle it.

Two weeks before, Hendrix had died.
Raymond shrieked on the phone to me,
All our slang seemed like a child's uneasy bravery.

I played their records
And felt again how they turned terror into a good time:
He was screechingly wry, she was throbbingly kind.
Like the GIs they had told us about in school
These people died so
Others could live—
        but we could have lived if they had lived.
Enjoying yourself was not a cause or manifesto

But an attitude—goosing the gods of ordinariness,
Outraging a day shift destiny.

If it was bad,
It was bad the way too much pathos or tequila was bad,
That blank bedrock of energy
When the singing and the sex were over
And you awoke imperfectly
To inhale a twitching cigarette,
A manager's obligations
And the personal echo
      of those anonymous, imploring fans.

Out in the cheering dark we remain.
We are still listening, but life is like death,
So strong it doesn't have to explain.

THOM GUNN

The Victim

Oh dead punk lady with the knack
Of looking fierce in pins and black,
The suburbs wouldn't want you back.

You wished upon a shooting star
And trusted in your wish as far
As he was famous and bizarre.

The band broke up, its gesture made.
And though the music stopped, you stayed.
Now it was the sharp things he played:

Needles and you, not with the band,
Till something greater than you planned
Opened erect within his hand.

You smiled. He pushed it through your shirt
Deep in your belly, where it hurt.
You turned, and ate the carpet's dirt.

And then not understanding why
He watched out with a heavy eye
The several hours you took to die.

The news was full of his fresh fame.
He OD'd ending up the same.
Poor girl, poor girl, what was your name?

JACK RIDL

Video Mama

My mother watches videos,
tapes them on the VCR, keeps
a list of her top twenty.
In the next room, her grandchildren
play, pretending they are rabbits.
On the wall, behind the TV,
she's hung family photographs:
her father, mother, mother's father,
aunts and uncles, cousins, two
great-grandfathers, and her children
and their children and her wedding
picture. Next to Cousin Dot,
is an autographed picture
of The Boss, Bruce Springsteen,
bare-shouldered, sweating.
Guitar slung across his thighs,
he watches her all day long.

To Marie Osmond

There you are again,
your crystal-perfect face
on the cover of the *Enquirer*.
It seems you're everywhere this Spring,
on more magazines than April has roses.
And yes, your series flopped, but you really are
more suited to the slit sequined dresses of NBC
than to *Family Circle* declarations of virginity.
Lips of a TV Venus should pucker, not pout.

And what a waste that the nine men you love,
hinted at in this week's *Star*, turn out
to be your father and eight brothers, that
the husband you dream of would be another perfect virgin.
Your daddy's Mormon domain is as barren
of life as his head is of hair; let *me* be your conquering
consort and you'll be a far richer heiress, when
the shadows of Utah's long Winter are fled,
and you stand alone on the Rockies, surveying
an ancient city of soft buildings, which transubstantiate
and interpenetrate in moon-aluminum evening, where warm
headlighted insects dance in circles, and golden
movie star men stand upright among beasts,
holding tokens of serpents, sunglasses, electric guitars.

RICHARD SPEAKES

Mama Loves Janis Joplin

It turns out you can have a daughter selling
Girl Scout cookies at the mall, own a freezer
closing in on what's left of the tater tots,
watch the soaps, and still roll joints
matter of fact as a stoned stare at the yearbook.
Maybe it wasn't supposed to be like this,
the magenta Indian bedspread over the years fading
to a pink without a pattern, so methodical
you could graph it,
                              the long swoon and slouch
that shows how you got from brown rice
to Bunny Bread, from getting busted to getting
appointed chairperson of a PTA committee.
But that's how it goes, or that's how it
gathered then sprawled, as if life's a wave
you catch and ride, the sort of Beach Boys fantasy
Hendrix meant to kill.
                              One day it sloshed
onto a beach where you watched kids scatter gulls,
your kids, their play with their good father.
Behind them the horizon said not to worry,
keep going and you come all the way back to yourself.
Today there is no then to now, no there to here,
but everywhere an edge, and from the other side
Janis shouts, screams, whispers, soothes then pounds.
Hope is the door you can kick down one day and
ease through the next, like raising a dimestore slip

past your hips, slick so maybe you won't notice
it comes off easy from practice.
                                        You lift it
as if it were his spirits, that one man the songs
always promise themselves, as we promise children
whatever it takes to keep them quiet. *Maybe,*
maybe, maybe, Janis sings with doubt's small prop,
so she can pretend she's being honest.
Play it loud, the horn section blasting us all
out of this mess of need, and sing the thrilling lie,
that one good man could put a stop to it.
Near the end,
                        you could hear her knowing
what nonsense it was, that she had only her memories
of the songs' making sense. You could hear her
going into that room, settling instead for good dope.
But what can you say, knowing these things?
Making dinner, fussing a child's hurt, nights
when you wrap your legs around your man . . .
like a back-up chorus of do-wah do-wah beauties,
you find the harmonies, and you sing along.

WALTER MCDONALD

Honky-Tonk Blues

Shoving another quarter home to make
jukebox stars keep singing at night
in Texas, I think of Uncle Bubba
chopping wood, heaving his bad back
to it, in town again for a weekend.

Chips flew from his axe like high notes.
Puffing, he hummed the same old
country and western tunes that kept him
fed and human, half the honky-tonk
clubs in Texas more like his home

than Lubbock. Aunt Myrtie lived alone
five months out of six, pedaling
a Singer sewing machine to stay
faithful, trying to spin gold
from cotton threads and telegrams

he wired her twice a week. Whatever
she sewed sold fast at auction
in the mall and the county fair.
Now Bubba lives alone in a trailer park
in Austin, bait for tornadoes,

his stove a butane heater he seldom
lights. He sits outside as late
as his neighbors let him, strumming,
humming old songs like a scab
he keeps picking at over and over,

no new tunes ever right
for ballads about a cruel
good-hearted woman who let down
her spun silk rope one night
and slid out of his arms forever.

DAVID ST. JOHN

Homage to Robert Johnson

*There's a hellhound
on my trail.*

Sometimes the moon
Rides these trees like a red feather
Walking its milk light through the branches
Onto these long beds of pine dust
And yellow needles

I sit on the porch scraping my boots
Over the rough boards

I used to sleep with a woman who swore
Each morning the anger rose in my bones like dew
That in my dreams I beat her
Like a coat
So I pushed my thumbs up beneath her cheekbones
Until she knew why all along this delta

The oil fires flared

Like the tracks kicked-up behind the devil's
New shoes
She sleeps with the child now I don't mind
I just sit up late on this porch

Watching that boy drive
Back and forth in his silver Terraplane
The boy with a face like a woman the voice
Of a hurt cat

Like the tine of a steel fork striking glass

I think I'll go to Amarillo
I know a hotel where the rooms open like memory

Onto fecund nights
Onto rains still blue or blouses empty
The vein's filament still lit in the crook of my
Elbow the spoon burned to a bruise

The asphalt roads quiver in the heat
Salvation setting like a moon in its last black
Spiraling range of sky

RICHARD SPEAKES

Heartbreak Hotel Piano-Bar

Okay. We're stuck with our lives and those
we can imagine, themselves cover versions of
the originals. But hum a few bars of any
old standard, this piano player gives you
a song unlike the one you know by heart.
The notes are there all right, but the way
they're on sheet music, along with the fourth verse
no one ever sings.
                          Maybe the song was meant to be
played just so, but I remember a tone, something like
one color feathered into another, the way rainbows
do blue to green. Fred said he couldn't play it,
said it isn't in the notes. Many tips later
I believed him. I remember the night I took that
and knew it—a revelation of the usual sort,
when you can see your needs because they
are lost in their work and can't be bothered.
I remember because it was the night I realized
my mind plays piano.
                          A song shared, but poorly—
it's like a crossroads to me now, a place where
our distances collide . . . and then go on.
But a piano, a chair, things between one nothing
and the next, they're crossroads too, like a woman
in your arms the first time. That's when I was
hearing the song as I trust Fred never to play it.
That's why I come here, for the music.

JOSEPH HUTCHINSON

Joni Mitchell

Water falls white on the white
washed stones, fingers
light on piano or the spine
of a lover.
Sobs and exultations,
the open mouths and eyes of astounded
houses, doves
dead in mid-air, a scatter
of leaves like torn astrologies.

With her voice full of swords and blossoms,
salt and blond honey, voice
like the ruffle of air off the tip
of the heron's wing,
she sings the scrawl of blood
and the fiery scripture
of nerves
written under the skin.

We've slept like mountains, but now
drum and saxophone swim
in our bodies,
hook-jawed salmon that leap
the black keys, dying
for the drowned genital stars,
their fine bones singing like tuning forks.

And there are guitars
overflowing like drunken goblets,

shiny sea-turtles dragging
inland, heavy with eggs. There are
sparrows dreaming in the cradles of her wrists,
and roses, and ashes, and oceans
collapsing on empty beaches, sliding
back helpless and rising again.

CHARLES LYNCH

Ancestral Echoes / Rap Music

Sunk in slate-gray plastic panels—
    grid with silvery dials, pushbuttons, screws—
    black speakers boom from humongous box
    strapped to bopping minstrel's shoulder

Teak neck roped gold,
chief of crew walks the talk   king   drum,
    prospects Dr. Ronald McNair Park party zone,
    spins hip-hop M.C.'s funky baritone

Toting sermon at a rebellious treble,
    summons down crowd who
        respon' en call, y'all
        chant boastful   banter   scat
        staccato rhyme   rhythm-prism riff
        get clap-happy double-time
            to bass syncopation rappers make
            mikeing gruff huff, slurred burp, sputter

Jam Master Dakari plays on it,
    mixes, cuts, and scratches,
    sand-dances electric chakere

FLOYD SKLOOT

The Everly Brothers

My brother thought they were freaks
of nature, voices fitting together
through some fluke of chemistry.
He said they might just as well
have been Siamese twins sharing
a heart or the Everly humpbacks.

My brother preferred Jerry
Lee Lewis and Chuck Berry.
He cackled at their antics,
battering mother's baby
grand with his fists when we
were alone and duckwalking
the hallway until our downstairs
neighbors hit their ceiling
with a broom. At night he worked
on his Elvis sneer while caking
his face with Clearasil.

I can still see my brother
rave as we rode four stories
up in the quaking elevator.
He offered me one frenzied
groove of Yakety Yak at the top
of his lungs when I tried
to sing. All I wanted was
his voice joining mine in
harmony. The song did not
have to be about faith in love.

DAVID GRAHAM

Father of the Man

Your daughter, fifteen, has drunk half a bottle
Of gin, passing out in the bushes.
Her boyfriend's car costs twice what your first house did.
Blood of your blood, heart root blossoming,
still she does not figure in this story.

For a more bitter car now squeals away.
The hair you've lost is not entirely gone:
see, it returns on your son's clenched jaw
as he plays air guitar in his bedroom,
his walls all Nazi regalia, his dreams
all wind-stunned and far from this sick village.
Yes, here is the hard seed you recognize.

No, he won't go to the ballpark with you.
He's tired of your beery friends, your tape deck
spewing Sixties junk, throbbing blue vein
rising on your temple. And old? He's never
seen such a decrepit father, when you've
tipped a few and begun leering at
the available wives, sometimes even
stripping your shirt off for volleyball. . . .

And you know that *grump grump* bass that rises
all evening from his basement hideout?
It's nothing but your sullen, well mapped fate.
It's all those wind-in-the-blood whiskey nights
you vowed never to forget or regret.
It's dust spraying as you popped your wheelies

through the vacant lot that's now a realtor's.

It's the open legs of your dream at last
beckoning—no, you can't leave her out now—
her prom-night giggle and hushed, skinny-dipping
waters you still feel throb in your belly.
Bass and drum, the synthesized wail rising
to the night trees—father, it's all you ever
hoped or could be, this welcome capsizing
and perfect acquittal. This shutout game
you'd never have trusted when you were your age.

ROBERT GIBB

Paul Butterfield, Dead at 44

All my friends are going, people,
and things just don't seem the same.
   —"Born in Chicago"

So the blues are again requiem
For one of their own. And who isn't?
As though these songs weren't really
Spirituals all along, the flesh's
Hurt and passion, and spirituals
Lullabies for the soul. As though
Bluesmen haven't known this from
The start—how through wailful choirs
Grief can be transfigured into
A kind of exultation, kin to joy,
Or stopped down like a flame to one
Fierce, tender burning.
                                    First time
I heard him, I thought an elephant
Was trumpeting, there was so much
Muscle to the sound. This evening
I listen once again to that song
Of nativity and its aftermath, but
Hear for the first time the pride
In its complaint. And when my son
Comes toddling into the room, drawn
By the harped chromatics, I lay down
What I can of pity, and take him up,
And we dance, together, in time.

BRUCE BERGER

Salad Days

Into the common bowl—
Lettuce, onion, lemon, olive oil, salt—
Your mother diced the bland
Irresistibly resilient lettuce stem,
Then with your helpless father held back as we,
Tines cocked for each
Pale eruption, feinted, stabbed,
Missed, breached, stilettoed,
Keeping score as, again and again
Daring each other's flesh, we heartward speared,
Me at your drummer's hand, you at my pianist's hand
That had to keep time with each other and,
Several hours a day, the rest of the band.

KAY MURPHY

The Girl with the Bad Rep

1. The Exile of Music

Flay the square with crowds.
Who reads the names of the dead?
A 21 gun salute at 18.
The sun boiling its way through the smoke
lifting the rotten fog.
Someone dreams of a picnic band concert,
horns glinting like bayonets, lawn chairs
paired over a sloping lawn.
A Greek theater family Sunday afternoon.
The smoke not yet dispersed,
    shots echo through the courthouse clock,
time stops for you.

2. A Bracelet of Razors

Waltz to electronic voices
speaking Mom   Dad   Love   Love that stuff.
Chubby   Count   Dizzy   Duke   Dusty   Fats
Little   Marvin killed by his father.
Satch   Smokey
Who knows where the R&R went that year?
A nest of needles in the hospital.
A fall off the wagon.
Dance fool! Dance
or drop dead. That's my sister
you're bringing back from the grave.

3. Why the Cur Laughed

Everything stopped just as I was.
We rolled together like thunder.
You came in spurts.
How holy can that be? The street
outside dips, silly with holes.
A man in a dress waves up to us,
fluttering fingers. He knows who I am.
Cars pass indifferently.
Not even young punks throw rocks but nod off
in different directions.
Her tail swings like a happy dog.

4. The Song of Bones

We shine in the skin, a skull and cross,
museum collection, dinosaur's demise,
animal treat. Digger's delight, deeply
exhausted, pick one like a flower,
rest your weary to the marrow.
A calcium deposit, old contention, hair bow,
nose piece, knock-kneed dread.
Ghost story in translation. One of the top
five symbols in a contemporary poem,
we lie with happiness, rhyme with stones,
fly with wings of light.
We're a flute, a fluke, a Piltdown forgery.

5. There's Nothing Like It

Something gonna happen, feel it
in your bones, the engine's hum.
Who knows, maybe it will all work out,
a work of art. White boats open
close the pavement, reconstructed teeth

for the visitation. Don't be so low
she said, Sister, who hasn't been on earth
since school let out. The window rolled down,
R&R like any other guy, over.
We found two streets safe to walk on
the map of my ribs. The rest mines,
pitfalls, balancing acts, a Georgia O'Keeffe
with meat. Oh yes, we took advantage
of your absence, we addressed sympathy's
envelopes,
we danced like fools through the ancestors.

ALISON STONE

Spofford Hall

I had to write my
Obituary,
And scream at a chair.

Once you say there is a God,
They give
Your hairspray back.

My counselor has
A record in six countries, and thinks
Billie Holiday's a man.

I have been called
"Whore" eleven times. Now a talk on self-esteem. I nap
Under the bed or in the bath. They make me
Wear my t-shirts inside out.

Today is visiting day.
Mom brings bagels and a rabbit
With a red felt tongue. Dad tries to execute
A hug.

There is not enough room for us all.
If the spread is creased, I get
A sad face on my door.

Naturally we talk about
My weight gain and the view.
The lake is freckled with dead fish.
Patients circle in pairs.

DOYLE WESLEY WALLS

The Summer the Beatles Went Over Seven Minutes on a Single

Death wasn't the only thing aboveboard in New Orleans.
Moss wasn't the only thing hanging down.
Strippers, emblems of shame, dressed
Bourbon St. in the trashy finery of
my junior high imagination.
My parents, good Baptists from Texas, had no desire
to go club hopping.
They wanted to drink the coffees, eat the seafood, visit
the sights, give their children some more of the education
travel affords.

Drunks, a world of lost sinners, beat on doors
at our Holiday Inn the first night, belting out their
sad song.

I went swimming under black Louisiana skies
and there in the pool met wet a girl my age
and her brother or cousin. Turned out they were
from New Orleans, lived just down the street.
I remember thinking
I could never have cheated a motel like that.

The girl's body would shimmy and shake
through the breakings of water
when I did revolutions off the diving board.
She would ride me
as I walked her into the deep.
She was under my skin because I didn't know

her name. She was the Queen of Wet. I floated,
a lump of dough in a vat of grease. I sank more gladly
than I ever have since under the weight of bourbon.

It was a week of dark evenings, thick with the night-lit
pool and frogs' legs, bass, shrimp, catfish,
beignets, and swimming underwater, woozy in the heat,
watching her with new fisheyes,
letting desire spawn in me, the fishes
growing to feed the multitude
of wants in me, diving back down, touching bottom,
surfacing with her thongs, one in my mouth, one
in my suit, baptizing myself in the faith
that it would all be there for the taking, and it was
going to be all right. All right. All right.

JAMES SEAY

Audubon Drive, Memphis

There's a black and white photo of Elvis
and his father Vernon in their first swimming pool.
Elvis is about twenty-one and "Heartbreak Hotel"
has just sold a million.
When he bought the house,
mainly for his mother Gladys they say,
it didn't have a pool,
so this is new.
The water is up to the legs of Vernon's trunks
and rising slowly as he stands there
at attention almost.
Elvis is sitting or kneeling on the bottom,
water nearly to his shoulders,
his face as blank and white
as the five feet of empty poolside at his back.
The two of them are looking at the other side
of the pool and waiting for it to fill.
In the book somewhere
it says the water pump is broken.
The garden hose a cousin found is not in the frame,
but that's where the water is coming from.
In the background over Vernon's head you can see
about three stalks of corn
against white pickets in a small garden
I guess Gladys planted.
You could press and point and say that in the corn
and the fence, the invisible country

cousin and mother, the looks on Elvis and Vernon's
faces, the partly filled pool, we can read
their lives together, the land
they came from, the homage they first thought
they owed the wealth beginning to accumulate,
the corny songs and films,
and that would be close but not quite central.
Closer than that is the lack
of anything waiting in the pool we'd be
prompted to call legend
if we didn't know otherwise.
They're simply son and father wondering if it's true
they don't have to drive a truck
tomorrow for a living.
But that's not it either.
What it reduces to is the fact that most of us
know more or less everything
that is happening to them
as though it were a critical text
embracing even us and our half mawkish
geographies of two or three word obituaries:
in the case of Kennedy, for example, I was walking
across a quad in Oxford,
Mississippi; King's death too caught me in motion,
drifting through dogwood in the Shenandoah.
As for Elvis,
there were some of us parked outside a gas station
just over the bridge from Pawley's Island
with the radio on.
That's enough.
I know the differences.
But don't think they're outright.
The photo is 1034 Audubon Drive, Memphis,
and then it's Hollywood,
still waiting for the pool to fill.

FLOYD SKLOOT

The Year the Space Age Was Born

That fall, when we shared a phonograph,
my brother returned one morning
and caught me playing his "Party Doll"
record, imitating Buddy Knox
with a baseball bat for my guitar.

I thought he was on his way to school.
From the bed where I stood lost in rock
n' roll, I watched him gather up news
reports of Sputnik, raging about
Russians beating us to space, screaming
he knew I knew not to touch his things.

Then how could I listen to the hits?
He'd be glad to give me lots of hits,
an even dozen audible hits
that would rocket me into orbit,
if he found me playing them again.
We shared the room, not what was in it.

What about air and what about light!
What about a slap across my face!

Now I often think of how it was
between us when the distance between
us was years instead of miles. Light years,
we used to say, when our eight years were
forever. Now old hits are the same
for both of us. People live for months

in space and ask that Mission Control
play "Party Doll" as their wake-up call.

My brother and I live a thousand
miles apart. Buddy Knox is touring
all year long out of Winnipeg, still
singing his one hit at 53,
a long way from his Happy, Texas,
home. I will admit we haven't left
that much behind ourselves. Only our
place of birth, the little space we shared.

DOROTHY BARRESI

Vacation, 1969

Brothers rolling around in the big back seat,
all elbows and skirmishes,
complaints roared across Mt. Rushmore,
that hard family portrait,
across the Badlands purple with heat.
Back home, black children looted fire hydrants
under sinus-grey skies.
Our trailer was a cracker box ready to jackknife
when my sister, good reader,
practiced her phonetics: nā' päm.

I think it was just outside Turlock, California
that I grew too sullen
for togetherness.
Rocking my new breasts in my arms,
I was conked out by hormones and Mick Jagger,
my face held in acne's blue siege.
So I pulled up oars early that August,
slept while the boys knocked heads
and my iron-eyed parents took turns
lashed to the wheel,
America, by God, filling the car windows.

KATHARYN HOWD MACHAN

In 1969

What were the secrets that we didn't tell?
Bold lyrics blared, drums throbbed a rhythm full
of wanting, cry of organ rose and fell,
and always the guitars wailed out to pull
us sweating through our adolescent fears.
Inside we kept to silences, you locked
in anger at your father's fists, my tears
saved tight for pillows when the whiskey knocked
the laughter from my mother's voice: the sound
of shame still louder for us all than rock
and roll. We danced, we smoked, desire found
the words to reach for sex—yet we made mock
of anyone who tried to make us say
what hurt. We lied; there was no other way.

JUDITH VOLLMER

Nursing the Sunburn

Only here that I roll my dope
in banana flavored papers and sip coffee
with a vibrator salesman. I'm finally
androgynous since I look like Neil Young
in mirrored sun glasses. This is the place
where I could have grown up to be
Isabelle Adjani with smoky eyes
& a body that would never want to wear
anything but black.
There's a baby pelican
on the back porch and Nina Simone's
on the stereo. Motor boats unzipping
the canal cost more than houses do
back home, and some restaurants
can only be reached by water.

The Intercoastal Waterway funnels the aroma
of open sewers,
and backs of ships in Biscayne Bay
are stacked with tractor trailers bearing
bumper stickers like, "I brake for nice tits,"
and "I honk for Jesus." In Miami Beach while rats
scrape across boulders inches from my
bare feet, I'm happy to find
a chunk of white coral and I'm happy
I'm going back to snow & to my own cold house
with firewood stacked up on the porch,
where everything is quiet:
only smoke & the small gray city outside.

SYDNEY LEA

Tempted by the Classical on Returning from the Store at Twenty below Zero

Weather in place of God.
Legends of power in the store
float thick, misshapen as ghosts
around any Mather. The gilded
register quaintly gongs
among children devoted to sugar,
plastic. The walls are sweet
with rhetoric: TRY OUR OLDE
NEW HAMPSHIRE MAPLE SYRUP,
or angel-faced hippies' clichés
of redemption: *Natural. Pure.*
Pure nature hisses through nailholes:
the wind is "sharp as a knife,"
the snow is "as tall as a steeple,"
the country "the last place God made."
Creosote clumps like sap
on the roof, outside. In idle
snowmobiles ("The Cat,"
"The Stinger") oil congeals.
Darkly. On television
a fool sings "You Light Up My Life."
Stuck to the truck's door handle,
wisps of heavy-fleshed thumb
come off to flitter from chrome
in the moon. The engine argues,

fires. The radio explodes
in the cab: Big Apple disco,
sex-electric. Barren
meadows glaze, untracked.
Hardwoods like frigid columns.
The floorboards are alabaster
with rime. Heart slows and whimpers,
set in a marbled coldness.
My memory's not what it was.
I paw at the dial to quiet
an ad: "Your Saving Place". . . .
Weak gratuitous beams
from my headlamps show a frieze:
two white coyotes turned to stone.
Perhaps there's some other salvation. . . .
The tarmac tells tonight
how easily it could brain
a man, despite the years,
Time's purchases, the lies:
the small stiff pile of condoms,
girls' blood, red as ideas
of summer, conversation
into the clogged telephone,
in which one offered his slogans—
"I love you," "I'm sorry"—or didn't,
the world of friendship's fetor,
the sprawling spring cotillions,
weddings, importunate children,
old folks in convalescent
"homes," fuel bills, cars.
I lose my words. Hard stars,
imperious, chip at my tumble
of hair, the dune of my skull,
embarrassing squalor of marrow
and meat. My fingers shoot
a spark of blue-near-silver.

In each myopic eye
a small moon settles and burns.
But I decline to brake
under the strait sharp sky.

JIM ELLEDGE

Household Gods

Tuned to 104.6 on the FM
dial, the boom box purrs Golden
Oldies I jerk awake to. You
turn beside me, to me, but turning,
wind tighter into sleep. "I
think it's great," you mumble, each
syllable and breath an array of
totem wrapped in haze—a logo
constructed some finer place than
this, plumb-bob perfect by no
light but the dial's
red rectangle.
              Horae lacrimae,
these hours strung midnight to 7:00's
alarm, each moment a stepping
stone across terrain where music
uncoils and rears to strike, where
wakefulness is goblin, pilgrim,
goblin again. The clutter of eras
packs each moment breathed,
each footprint left, while
Johnny Angel attends your heart like
those household gods Caesar's
Rome raised to block each
portal against barbarian, evil
eye, famine.
            That land you stride through

stretches ahead, behind, buoyed between
lungs, nestled within the rib cage.
For me, it lies as uncharted as
those vast lands cartographers
fixed onto maps millennia ago, pastel
jig-saw pieces they labeled
Terra incognita, and where,
between each vaguely boundaried
blotch, they printed in their best
hand warnings to mariners then, after:
HERE, FRIEND, BE DRAGONS.

DAVID TRINIDAD

"Monday, Monday"

Radio's reality when
the hits just keep
happening: "I want
to kiss like lovers
do. . . ." Why is it
I've always mistaken
these lyrics for my
true feelings? The
disc jockey says it's
spring and instantly
I'm filled with such
joy! Is it possible
that I'm experiencing
nature for the first
time? In the morning
the sun wakes me
and I am genuinely
moved, almost happy
to be alive. For a
couple of weeks it'd
been getting a little
bit brighter every
day. I wasn't aware
of this change until
the morning I noticed
the angle at which
the light hit your

GQ calendar, fully
accentuating the aus-
tere features of this
month's male model, as
I sat in the kitchen,
in your maroon robe,
and waited for my tea
to cool. I was thinking
about my feelings, about
how much I loved the sun
when I was a child and
how I loved the dark
as well, how thrilling
it was to lie in bed
on windy nights and
listen to the sound of
bushes and branches being
thrashed about outside.

Actually, that's what
I was thinking while
you were making the tea.
I was staring at the
calendar, at the smoke
from the tip of my
cigarette as it drifted
in the sunlight toward
the open window, when
you set the steaming
fifties-style cup in
front of me. Was it
at this point that
my manner changed?
Your gesture reminded
me of innumerable
mornings spent with

my parents in the pink
kitchen of my childhood.
I remembered my mother,
how she always wore her
gaudy floral bathrobe
and shuffled about in
her bedroom slippers as
she dutifully served us
breakfast. My father
sat alone at one end
of the table, his stern
face all but hidden
behind the front page
of the *Los Angeles Times*.
They seldom spoke. I
felt the tension between
them, watched with sleep-
filled eyes as he gave
her the obligatory kiss
on the cheek, then
clicked his briefcase
shut and, without a word,
walked out the door.

As I was getting dressed,
you grabbed me, kissed
me on the lips, said
something romantic.
I left your apartment
feeling confused, got
on the freeway and
inched my way through
the bumper-to-bumper
traffic. I was confused
about sex, about the
unexpected ambivalence

which, the night before,
prompted my hesitancy
and nonchalant attitude:
"It's late," I said,
"Let's just sleep."
The cars ahead of me
wouldn't budge. I
turned on the radio and
started changing stations.
I was afraid I would
always be that anxious,
that self-obsessed, that
I might never be able
to handle a mature
relationship. Stuck on
the freeway like that,
I was tempted to get
into it, the pain and
the drama, but the mood
soon passed. (After
all, it *is* spring.)
At last, traffic picked
up and I enjoyed the
rest of the drive, kept
the radio on all
the way to work and
listened to all those
songs, though I finally
realized those songs
were no longer my feelings.

ROCHELLE NAMEROFF

"California Dreaming"

I don't believe in anything
this early in the morning
in my cold bones apartment,
the sun now a foreigner,
and the friendly radiator hiss
withheld until the law says ON.
Instead there is a warning
near the mailbox: Get 4-6 blankets,
thick socks and thermal underwear.

Get used to stinginess—it's good
for the soul. The rent will rise
anyway, unlike the sun. So get
a move on. Turn on a song.
But it's only October
and I'll die here in the snow.
I don't want to sing right now.
I want to climb into a hot
soapy tub in California,

smell the eucalyptus on the ground,
drink the proper snobby wines
and live forever.

DAVID ST. JOHN

California

Who do you love?
—Bo Diddley

My last night in California
She got up from the broken bed
Standing naked a moment
Before pulling on her boots only
Her boots with their razor toes
And lizard skins
Before pulling back the drapes
That covered the dusty window of
Our small room in the old
Stucco motel
       the window
A floor-to-ceiling checkerboard
Of opaque and clear panes
She looked out at the trucks passing
In the rain down the old section
Of highway 99
       the rainbows
Of the spilled oil and neon mixing
On the rain-glazed asphalt
Of the parking lot
Maybe she was thinking of a moon
In the teeth of the Sierras
A moon setting in the mountains
Beyond her father's ranch
Where it would be

Clear above these storm clouds
Maybe of her husband just
Getting up to the late news and his
Shift at the mill
But as I reached by the bed to the low
Table where I'd thrown my watch
And before I could say *Come here*
Don't worry or any dozen stupid things
She began to rock slowly back on the heel
Of one boot snapping out the other
Like a whip kicking out one
By one the small
Square panes of the window
Each echoing ricochet of glass louder
Than the drone of the trucks outside
And as the lights of the room
Next door flashed
On a moment their sudden glare
Hitting the windshields of the cars
Nosed up in front of every door
I grabbed her around the waist
And pulled her back onto the bed
Her fingernails slicing
The whole length of my cheek
Three long parallel lids
Of skin opening as the blood ran
Down onto my chest
                    I held her
Until the lights next door went off
As the sound of the rain the trucks
And the night grew
Now when I go back to California
I don't ask where she is
                    or why
I only know it wasn't the risk
That kept us meeting in motels

In the bars of Chinese restaurants
It was simply the desire to be
Desired
            the lie
The good lie told softly in the dark
Each night to keep believing
You're lucky
            more lucky than most
                        that if
The world holds many dreams at least
One of them holds you

ROBERT LONG

"What's So Funny 'bout
Peace, Love and Understanding"

At the party she said
"You only want what you can't have,"
As you smashed into a locked door.
Give up. The telephone's exploding
With all the wrong numbers, and,
Yes, the blank wall's fascinating,
So who needs sleep?

Here's someone breathing
Appropriate exhortations in your ear,
Here's someone else
With a twelve-in-one knife,
Here's the guy in the deli
Calling you "sir"
As he wraps the roast beef.

I remember adolescence.
It went by in a blur of hallucinogens,
Peace signs, and speechlessness: days,
Hot beach, then the beach at night:
That perfect sleep sound,
And the stars,
Like push pins in really lovely material.

"When You Wish Upon a Star That Turns into a Plane"

—The Replacements

My clothes are standing up without me
though it's just the bus is here,

the noise of people pulling things
into line. I don't want a ride

but the driver leans out the door
as if to pull me into heaven.

So I light a french fries wrapper
and think: Go away, and he does,

the door folds shut and woosh, there
goes the bus.

A bum sits down and cups
a cigarette that isn't there—

he shakes his hand and takes a drag.
The air is brown around us, like an old

snapshot, and I spend three minutes
trying not to breathe, just sipping now and then.

Then I walk to Sunset Boulevard,
where on good days with God willing I can

hitchhike all the way to the beach.
I am certain the sea will rise one day

and drive its way inland, but not today.
Today will end with a colorful dusk,

a stain the length of California
fading as the sun goes down.

When I was small there was always a meal
that everyone agreed on, and the stars

falling over the city.
I'd watch the ocean from my parents' roof

and Catalina on somedays, like a fist
above the smog. It's 14 miles and three

transfers from here to Pasadena,
and my mother has said on the phone

that she loves me regardless of what
I'm taking. What am I taking?

I remember who I am and where I'm from
but I don't remember why.

This is nothing to cry about
so I don't. I sit down

and wave past another bus.
I watch myself flicker in its windows.

JUDITH ORTIZ COFER

Seizing the Day

You are traveling within the boundaries of your time together,
finite as a glass cube, within which
you do not plan
past this afternoon, this night. Inside,
the autumn sun,
infused with white light and a little heat,
strokes the windshield of the car,
underneath the peaked shade of mountains.

You are listening
to a top one hundred countdown on the radio. She says
"Satisfaction" will be on top—"Satisfaction"
always is.

As you sear these roads in your haste to get somewhere
you have never been before,
you notice the leisurely pace
of free lives in their familiar routines:
how an old man, digging in his mailbox
for news of a world he does not believe in,
stares at your face hurtling past
with the hooded eyes of a potential witness.

And how a young couple, facing each other across a table
near a window in a small cafe,
raise glasses of wine to their lips, oblivious
to the way, flashing by,

you have stolen their souls with your eyes.

DAVID KELLER

After Supper

In the last light I drove
the inconsequential roads leading home, full of red wine
and fresh peach shortcake,
two wonderful salads and hot dogs and the first corn
and someone's lemon cream puffs and more wine,
and my clothes were rough with glue and the dirt
from the work, crossing the anonymous land,
its secret farms and the bushes full of fireflies,
happiness lighting the air.
This might have been the last unspoiled day
of them all, the work and the laughter
passed hand over hand
in the sunlight full of cats and starlings.
Tonight the horses left out to play,
and the darkness over the final daylilies
at the road sides are an invitation
to accept or not, like sleep, with no regrets.
On the radio a song from the Fifties played.
It used to be one of my favorites,
not for the words, but those terrific harmonies
that make them end too soon.
Everyone loved me, and that spendthrift warmth escaping
like bubbles into the solemn and holy wine.
Nothing to wish for and not be given,
for once, greedy as the little girl

at the swimming pond, naked, enquiring
of her favorite aunt if she had
chocolate, and then, insistent, "Well,
do you got any at your house?"

DOROTHY BARRESI

How It Comes

Like the small sound
from across chain link, your briarhopper
neighbor taking a long pull on a Bud,

then spritzing a little on his hibachi
that smokes like an old box camera,
and spraying, too, his pale wife

wearing her zebra-print halter
over breasts full of sway and collapse,
who ricochets

back and forth, back and forth,
pink burger meat between her palms
with such rapt devotion

you see for the first time
what he saw all those summers ago
in the parking lot of the 7-11,

and why this afternoon the Grateful Dead
work their sweet pain just right
on a radio propped in a bathroom window, and why

this hound wears a bandanna and keeps falling
in love with himself in a new way
in a pond of dust—

joy's perennial wild card fan,
obedient to the only words that matter:
Catch! Attaboy!

So that when the delicious gift comes
he will be ready, though it comes
without warning,

like trust after a long uneasiness;
as when you were a child
and sleep took you mid-sentence

under the dome light and low
talk of fireworks going silver to blue in another town, faroff;
and your mother with a cool hand

on your father's sunburned neck as he drove.
The way fidelity still begins
in the backseats of the great, generous
muscle cars of the sixties.

DANA GIOIA

Cruising with the Beach Boys

So strange to hear that song again tonight
Travelling on business in a rented car
Miles from anywhere I've been before,
And now a tune I haven't heard for years
Probably not since it last left the charts
Back in L.A. in 1969.
I can't believe I know the words by heart
And can't think of a girl to blame them on.

Every lovesick summer has its song,
And this one I pretended to despise.
But if I were alone when it came on,
I turned it up full-blast to sing along—
A primal scream in croaky baritone,
The notes all flat, the lyrics mostly slurred—
No wonder I spent so much time alone
Making the rounds in Dad's old Thunderbird.

Some nights I drove down to the beach to park
And walk along the railings of the pier,
The water down below was cold and dark,
The waves monotonous against the shore.
The darkness and the mist, the midnight sea,
The flickering lights reflected from the city—
A perfect setting for a boy like me,
The Cecil B. DeMille of my self-pity.

I thought by now I'd left those nights behind,
Lost like the girls that I could never get,

Gone with the years, junked with the old T-Bird.
But one old song, a stretch of empty road,
Can open up a door and let them fall
Tumbling like boxes from a dusty shelf,
Tightening my throat for no reason at all
Bringing on tears shed only for myself.

ROBERT WRIGLEY

For the Last Summer

That summer with a thousand Julys
nothing mattered but the sweat on a girl's chest,
the sun's crazy blue weather, and a young man's
hands electric with want. The wind
above convertibles sighed in the cottonwood leaves,
the stars were stars and the moon ached
in its own silver heaven. He was king
of the swath a train whistle cut.

Crazy for speed, he held the girl and the wheel
and plummeted toward the bottom-lands,
foundry lights ablaze in the distance,
and war let him sing the songs he swore
he'd never forget. That summer
of week-long nights, blossom-dark,
fragrant with dew and a dust
as fine as milled flour, he dreamed.

And his dreams were all glory and light,
line-drives that never fell, his friends
his friends forever, and war
let him sleep until noon and wake
with the scent of his girl around him,
remembering the night before—
how he sang of a loss he couldn't imagine,
of broken hearts he could almost believe.

That summer with a thousand Julys
the sun going down each afternoon was more

beautiful than the day before, the factory smoke
vermilion and rust in its slant, and the night-
hawks like needles stitching the darkness down.
Nothing smelled as sweet as the gasoline
he pumped, nothing arced so cleanly
as the shop-towels he tossed toward their baskets.

The world rode shotgun and reclined
on the seat of his car, lovely in the glow
from the dash lights, soft and warm,
and he knew what it meant to adore. War
let him dawdle there, virtuoso of the radio,
king of the push-buttons, and all that played
for him, in the only hours of his life he ever knew
as his own, was music, music, music.

KEVIN STEIN

First Performance of
the Rock 'n Roll Band *Puce Exit*

If *puce* were sound not color,
  it would be us: Deep Purple,
though more confused and discordant,

our guitars tuned in electric ignorance
  of tone, key, each other—the word
puce derived from the Latin for "flea,"

as appropriate for pests in the hides
  of neighbors—our raucous weekend practice,
pubescent groupies lingering on basement steps,

first on the block to show hearing loss,
  first to wear paisley with polka dots.
And *exit*, of course, because music is

our ticket out. It's Peggy Wasilewski's
  fourteenth birthday party, a real gig,
her parents too cool, or simply so new

to America they're expecting something
  with accordion and banjo, not the freight
we unload from my father's beige Chevy:

amps, mikes, drums, Christmas color wheels
  for visual effect. We set up in the dirt
floor garage, our amps a wall of sound

maybe knee high across the left bay.
  Everything's plugged into a quad outlet

above the single ceiling bulb. Orange wires

cascade around us like a waterfall
   of blown fuses. We start, start over,
and start again, until we get right

the three drumstick beat and launch into
   an 18 minute version of "Satisfaction."
I'm howling "I can't get no!" even though,

in eighth grade, I'm not sure what it is
   I can't get any of, but it's something,
I am sure, I need as badly as any guy

ever needed anything, like "voice lessons,"
   the drummer screams. On break, we play
spin the bottle, Peggy flicking her tongue

and my choking with surprise, with glee,
   with adolescent resolve to improve
on the next round, which never comes.

Police arrive to pull the knotted plug
   and send us scurrying for the bushes,
guitars around our necks, though no one

is drunk or stoned on anything other than
   the rush of innocence soon to take a turn,
accelerating around the corner like Peggy,

three years later, first night with license
   and the family station wagon, her eyes
on the lit radio dial and not on the barber,

my barber, trudging home in rain, the scissors
   in his breast pocket soon to puncture
his heart beneath her tire's worn tread.

But none of that has happened to happen.
   It's spring, and the bushes we hunker in
make riotous bloom. They smell of sachet,

cheap pink tins scenting my mother's floral
    dressing table. Or maybe it's Peggy,
her breath against my still whiskerless face,

cops' flashlights, cymbals hissing as they spill
    in puffs of dust, and neither of us
in a hurry to leaven this sweet bouquet.

BRUCE SMITH

How Garnett Mims and the Enchanters Came into Your Life

The scent of pencil, a house full
of felt erasers and tacks your father carried home
each day from school. This stinks,
this long division, this history.
If only they'd play
"Duke of Earl" or "Lucille," yeah, "Lucille"
for you now, you'd forgive the lashing
every afternoon from the tails of commas. If only
"Sea of Love" would come through the grid
of this maroon transistor you hollowed out
Silas Marner in hardbound for, shaving away
plot and parts of your thumb and fingerprint
with his blue blades. Upstairs,
you wring the gooseneck lamp with both hands
and point it at the school board's surplus desk.
You're in the margins of your text, white
and slick as hoods of Pontiacs you'll take her
home in, past your father's house,
her books in the back on yours like sets
of fractions. You'll hit the black teeth on the dash,
and before the falsetto leaves
the static cardboard throat of radio
and leaps like a tongue in the ear,
you'll say to her, "Garnett Mims
and the Enchanters."

RONALD WALLACE

Smoking

I'm holding my cigarette out the car window,
hoping it will burn down faster
so I won't have to smoke it, the orange
tip sparking in the dark, turning to ash.

I'm fourteen, riding in the front seat
with a woman who should know better,
the pastor's son feeling her up
as her hands grip the wheel.

Oh grow up, they said, shoving
the Winstons at me with a match,
and I, too shy or stupid to protest,
did. We're riding through

this long night of adolescence,
Buddy Holly and the Big Bopper flopping
somewhere overhead, the future
stretched out filmy and seductive

on the bed of our separate thoughts:
the driver with our lives tight in her hands;
the pastor's son praying his way into her bra;
my cigarette and my anger burning on

so long that thirty long years later,
after cancer and car accidents
have had their way with them,
they're still there, cruising along

the side streets of my memory,
lighting me up again and again
every time I try to put them down.

KELLY CHERRY

Late Afternoon at the Arboretum

Riding along in my automobile.
My baby beside me at the wheel.
                              —Chuck Berry

The lilacs are in bloom
and the lake that was ice
is water green as crème
de menthe. Flowering Scotch broom

tugs at the eye, Yellow
Brick Road-style. I hold
your hand; your hands, the wheel. . . .
Are we saying hello,

good-bye, something in between?
The car is a Pontiac
station wagon; it's parked
in a very pastoral scene,

and as the sun enflames
the flowers, and the sky
above the arboretum
flares, then dims, making the names

of the trees difficult
to read, I study your face
in profile, now thinking
what dear Ruth had said, exult-

ing in her conscience, to
Naomi: Wherever

you go, I will come along.
　　　Here amid the alien heather
　　　and words from an old song,
I say her words, to you.

MICHAEL MCFEE

First Radio

A plastic transistor from Japan,
aqua, with black vinyl straps, some chrome trim,
an ear-sized speaker, dials like nails—
perfect in the pocket as a pack of cigarettes,
its hidden heart pulsing over mine.

At lunch, at recess, on the bus,
each fall I'd strain to crack the glamorous code
of the World Series, pinching bright flags
of foil around the bent antenna,
hoping to attract Mantle or Koufax or Gibson.

And at night, planted under my pillow
like a tooth, like a magic seed,
I'd fall asleep to top-40 big-city deejays
bouncing off cloud cover thousands of miles away,
better than any answered prayer.

PAUL ZARZYSKI

Hurley High

Though the nuns had dubbed us Crusaders
in the war against puberty, we gladly lost
to testosterone and Pabst
Blue Ribbon rumbling in our blood. We sang
the dirty version of "Louie Louie"
gung ho with elocution
we learned from Coach Wick,
W.W. II English-teaching marine
who recited "The Locker Room Charge
of the Light Brigade" like God, Himself,
pounding home to Moses how to block
for the power sweep. We cruised
the drag of a no-horse town
lit by aurora borealis and beer-sign
neon twisted into images
rioting inside us, our hearts
like tin cups raked
across our ribs. What terrific lust
we mixed with hope, with first sex
to alto sax and electric guitar—
brass horns and chromed cars
we cocked our smooth faces toward
while combing full heads of hair. We lived for hits,
six-packs, and the third duce
kicking-in down the s-curved river road
to Litzer's, where we flashed
our fake I.D.'s across the bar at Blind Ed,

blew Lucky Strike smoke-rings and rocked
wild on raw fun, just to pass
for 18 on a Friday night in 1966
when Friday night meant living,
and living meant sinning 'til dawn.

DAVID GRAHAM

Jesus Never Sleeps

Downstairs neighbors quicken
    each morning before we wake—

Jesus-rock litany, gospel aerobics
    rising through our mattress

like heat from winter's
    sullen garden.

Their joyful noise banishes fat.
    I see them toned

and electric as the guitars
    they haul to weekend revival,

trim and unflappable
    as game show hosts.

What blameless sport, to feel
    the beat in your bones

and call it God! Here
    to declare moral joy

in these corruptible bodies,
    these latter days.

Our sleep, though—we cannot
    love another's glee

rousting us from languid
    heartfast dreams,

and blear as we are we curse
  each tribal thump.

Yet who if not some antic god
  unglues our eyes, opens

our mouths to sabbath naming,
  and thrusts these two

nonbelievers into their own
  bodies' good news?

MICHAEL WATERS

The Burden Lifters

At least you left me the green
　　dial of the radio
　　　　sending forth its watery

light as I listened
　　to the all-night talk
　　　　shows till, bored with G

spots, vigilantes, the midnight
　　madness at Crazy Eddie's,
　　　　I tuned in the gospel

station, letting Willis Pittman
　　and his Burden Lifters
　　　　undo the damage of too

much talk—their harmonies
　　soared above New York,
　　　　held back the endless

babble of traffic, reduced
　　the hubbub of static
　　　　to a hush. In the back-

ground rose the sound
　　of women weeping, trudging
　　　　to the altar to be touched

by some euphoric preacher
　　for the sake of the souls
　　　　of their junk-ridden sons.

How many phone calls did I make,
    prayer aprons purchase
        from Reverend Ike, a host

of DJs spanning the seaboard,
    wanting someone to bless
        the hurt away, lift

my burden, let me groan,
    Lord, into the black
        telephone till dawn

eased down its light,
    gentle fingers upon
        my godforsaken shoulders?

SIDNEY BURRIS

On Living with a
Fat Woman in Heaven

The point is not that Troy
burned, but that fire-
light, before the fall, glanced
from shafts of drawn swords;

I left McDonald's today
wondering about that.
If the overweight woman
in purple and I are headed

for the same place, to bivouac
together on a gleaming plain
of ceramic tile with colored
grout, then perhaps I need

to say a few things about
my expectations: my agnostic
beliefs, a parry to her faith,
I could drop; my hunger

for all things invisible
would have to go, but I want
her to know that faced
with the early darkness

of winters in heaven,
I will light my lamp
without respect and snuff it

when I please; furthermore,

I will surround myself
with music—rock, no reggae,
a smattering from the early
nineteenth century (German),

and bluegrass if I can lay
my hands on a jar of liquor.
These terms are not negotiable.
The odds that I will see her

tomorrow at lunch are good,
but not better than the odds
that we will die, and, before
we have placed our last orders,

I thought we should square
these differences, then come out
staring, strangers once more,
but confident, we now agree,

that the full flesh of our strong
arms balances the weight-
less shadows of our fate.

JUDITH BERKE

Fifties Rock Party, 1985

The big living room is crowded,
but the group is playing "Heartbreak Hotel"
and she asks her husband to dance.
Not that that song means
anything to her,
but all of a sudden . . .
the blue lights, and the beat—
though it's not right. Not slow enough.
Come on and dance, she says,
remembering how she would try to teach him:
one and *two* and: so simple
really. . . . '56
and she puts a coin in the slot
at the Italian restaurant.
Let's just try this, she says,
meaning right there, in front of the jukebox,
she remembers. She's pulling him up
and he's looking embarrassed,
his face smooth and well-
mannered as Ike's the week before
on the cover of *Life.*
She buys the record and dances to it
by herself, when he's not there.
"Hound Dog." Elvis, from the waist up,
on TV. Things going by
smooth. Pleasant. That's the way her head
remembers it: the way Pat Boone

sang Elvis's songs: just the *notes* of them.
The way in this blue light
even her husband looks a little
wild, like Elvis.
That woman they met
who sang in a choir down in Tennessee.
Thought she was singing only
for heaven.

GARY SOTO

Heaven

Scott and I bent
To the radio, legs
Twitching to The Stones,
Faces wet, arms rising
And falling as if
Trying to get out or
Crawl the air—the
Air thick with our
Toweled smells.

                It's
'64, and our room
And its shaft of dust,
Turning, is all
There is—though Mamma
Says there's the car
To wash, the weeds,
The grass and garbage
Tilting on the back steps.
"Yeh, yeh," we scream
Behind the closed door,
And boost the radio
To "10" and begin
Bouncing on the bed,
Singing, making up
Words about this girl,
That car, tears,
Lipstick, handjives

[186]

In alleys—bouncing
Hard, legs split, arms
Open for the Lord,
Until Scott can't stand it
And crashes through
The screened window
And tumbles into a bush,
His shoulders locked
Between branches,
His forehead scratched,
But still singing,
"Baby, baby, o baby."

CHRISTOPHER GILBERT

Enclosure

After Howlin' Wolf

Mad daddy like mule
kickin' in someone else's stall,
rocks the home's premise.
Knocks at the front door,
teasin' the back door wide,
bends his broodin' voice
in African slang.
Mud-faced feelin' oozes
heart of devilbird,
parts them rural teeth
and blows off steam, a-crowin'
AOH, HOOO, HOOO, HOOOOHEEEE—
so-called back-door man
singin' in his rooster shoes
said, AOH-HOOO, HOOO HOOOOHEEEE.
Red black daddy cock
puttered in the 70's,
but sixty years of moanin'
dixie bottom blues—
was his prankish testament
how he howled his life.
Love was his calling,
said, *the girls'll understand.*
Spoke his trance-like line,
woke the dollgirl sleep
singin' AOH-HEEE, HOOO, HOOOOHEEEE.
WHA-HEEE, WHA-HEEE, HOOOO.

And when it's all done
the feeling leaves by the window,
rides the last-night dream.
The last guitar line
eeries outside the record—
spirit has no home.

The twelve-bar blues form,
the south, or Chicago,
or some woman's man
never got his number—
a man singin' his wretched roots
never sings at home.

Mud-faced vowels bred
in morning, rollin' along
the road thru his dead age,
chant of distant land
his only closeness. Trance-blue
breath, the drifter's home.

ROBERT PHILLIPS

The Death of Janis Joplin

October 4, 1970

Oh, Lord, won't you buy me
a Mercedes-Benz!

Because she was a white girl
    born black-and-blue,
because she was outsized victim
    of her own insides,
because she was voted
    "Ugliest Man on Campus,"
because she looked for something
    and found nothing—
    she became famous.

"Tell me that you love me!"
    she screamed at audiences.
They told. Fat Janis wouldn't
    believe. Twenty-seven,
a star since twenty-four,
    she tried to suck, lick,
smoke, shoot, drip, drop,
    drink the world.
    Nothing worked.

Bought a house, a place
    to go home to.
Bought a dog, something to give
    love to. Nothing worked.

Jimi Hendrix died, Janis cried:
  "Goddamn. He beat me
to it!" Not by much. Three weeks
  later she joined him.
  Part of something at last.

ALBERT GOLDBARTH

People Are Dropping Out of Our Lives

Joplin's voice, edged like a crack
in glass, breaks
out from the window and falls
two floors to the cold
campus night.
Across the empty street
one man stopped mid-step
listens attentively in the dim
verge of my peripheral vision.
Nameless, face
half-shadowed and form hunched
anonymous under windbreaker, he
and I balance
our sides of a city block.
Tenuous relationship.
We breathe, we form a spatial border.
In space we define, shape shifts
foot to foot and pocket to pocket.
As he exhales
a long black line of night
plumbs my throat for its measure.

Song:
hemorrhages up over Joplin's lips
and hits curbing. Litter:
cans, packs, crumpled cups
accept her flow and fill

beneath our footfalls like flasks
of invisible blood
from dead friends and lost lovers.
People are dropping out of our lives.
Pieces of constellation are missing.
And now, this man,
at his disappearance back
into flat shadow, now
as lamplight and real estate realign
to compensate for his physical absence,
now in that hole
attracting me across the street,
Joplin's words—like coal
never made it to diamond—
smoke the saffron-and-red-hot West Coast blues
from a black metallic brazier.

Nobody near. The house at my back,
my house, is all stoop and sill, all
exit. All panes have a shatter-pitch.
Nobody near. And only the rapid
passing flasher suddenly shines
fingerprints onto my blank window.
By that second of whorls, I know them,
angels of the night.
And, nobody near, and Linda playing
up and down my spine with her ghost hands,
I sing
past midnight with the choir:
Jimi Hendrix, Brian Jones, Jim Morrison,
and Janis. We sing,
the streets don't know what to do with it,
Linda's hands know all the notes,
a high one, a rising falsetto, the scales

tip in the sky and go for broke,
the star, the guitar, the shrieks
go higher, the hands go
capo up my neck.

DAVID BOTTOMS

Homage to Lester Flatt

Troublesome waters I'm fearing no more. . . .

Five seasons without traveling to a festival, without walking
into a field and hearing that voice.

And now after a long spell of rain, I step off my porch
and walk toward the river,
remembering the last time I saw Lester Flatt,
how thin he looked and sick
as he sat back in a lawn chair under the slouching pines
of Lavonia, Georgia,
and scribbled his name on the jackets of records.

How do the roots chord, Lester?
And the click beetle and the cricket, the cicada, the toad,
what harmonics do they sing in the high grass?

All of those voices
want me to praise your remarkable voice—

Tonight little sparks are winking in the fields, and the dead
are combing the edge of the forest, their arms
full of campfires.
Tonight the dead are building a stage under a funeral tent
and blowing the dust off banjos.
Tonight, for you, the dead are shaking the worms
from their ears.

Lester, singing whatever we want to about the dead
is the easiest thing in the world.
Believing it the hardest.

So this is where I stop, in this wet grass.
This is the river we're all troubled by, where the storm wash
rattling the bank echoes the tenor of our lives.

DAVID WOJAHN

Buddy Holly

What there's been of winter moves away,
and after dawn it's warm again, another easy thing
to sentimentalize. I walked this morning with the dog
around a tiny, artificial lake,
among swans and eucalyptus, and read of Buddy Holly
in the Sunday *Globe*. Dead twenty years,
his shattered glasses from the plane crash rediscovered
in a county morgue locker in Clear Lake, Iowa.
We talked of this, Hank and I, over beers
and underdone chicken, and nights when he drinks

alone in his house, Hank plays Buddy Holly until dawn.
How much, he asked last night, would those glasses
be worth today? I told him thousands, thousands.
How much can we remove from the dead
for our private, selfish use? Buddy Holly died younger
than I am today. We dusted off the old LPs
and tried as best we could to mourn him.
He once said he wanted to come back
from the dead—he and his child bride—as swans.
Because they're beautiful. Because they're mates for life.

There's Hank's wife in the photo
before her death, before the unappeasable lingering.
Sammy in her arms in Boston. Hank's taught Sammy
to sing Buddy Holly, in a voice that makes you certain
he understands, to stand in a chair and hoot
and mime a perfect, electric guitar: moonlit dance pavilion,

the wind now hushed, the reverie of moments
when everything beyond the singer stills. And only
the dead are breathing, their hands cupped gently
to whisper, again, their names into our ears.

VAN K. BROCK

Sphinx

Driving west in the afternoon,
Tallahassee to Tupelo
and Memphis, through Montgomery,
Birmingham, all that history,
to see why the papers and tube
are all converging on Elvis
with people all over the world,
on his first death day,
the sun at my back,
because you are there,

I'm inquiring after miracles
in the city of the Phoenix and Sphinx,
to observe what rises where garbage
is still the provender of the poor
and Kings still die for our dreams,
and ten miles west of you,
where a Beetle was crushed by a truck
in monsoon rain, lights flash around
a poncho, another body bag.
How fragile bodies seem.
And according to the rules for drivers,
I risk my life to write this
as I drive alone in my car,
watching the road through rain.

And you are not even a goddess,
though more alive in your absence

than any mortal could be.
And even if you were dead,
I would still talk to you,
not caring what people would say,
should they study me.

RICHARD SPEAKES

Patsy Cline

Much of what moves us is wrong, our hearts
the fools of ancient orders, dressed hilariously
in case nothing else is funny. Otherwise we're Lear

but with less impressive credentials,
and of the madness our choices offer—it seems
petty, deserving less nature's full-throated storm

that says of Lear's woes, *God damn right,*
deserving more the weather at the mall, a drone
and a light that takes Valium religiously.

What we have left in us, of nature and a discord
that is the storm's right mingling summation in a
clapped flash of light . . . it's a woman, a man.

And if the heart too thoroughly adores its own
kitsch grandeur, like an overdone theater, gaudy
and gimmicky in its yearnings for an audience,

still, its dramas are elegant: from the chair onstage
a man simply rises as it dawns on him, as they say,
a phrase that suggests we are planets rolling

in and out of light, not our own small selves when
we suddenly see it, what was right there all along,
like a force we would ignore. She doesn't love him,

that's all, and planets fall into the sun. . . .
Much as we move through air, we look past the tinsel's
rapture for a post, the clumsy hope that velvet

will make a bench seem posh, our rabble,
even our minds all hushed. We watch people
we could be, will be, and we are moved.

Eight Ball

Every time I tried to put the eight ball
in a corner pocket, memory knocking feebly
at the door on such a night, every time I scratched,
I looked up to see the same drops of rain
repeating themselves outside, while inside, the air
full of the gypsy smoke Lorca would have sung to,
they were never going to stop dancing, not going
to stop feeding quarters to the jukebox
to hear Willie Nelson and Ray Charles do
"Seven Spanish Angels." These were Lorca's old peasants
in those poems about desperate love,
death in red suspenders and new jeans,
hope, maybe older, in a big frill blouse,
doing the two-step for half the night, celebrating love
while time lingered over a mint julep at the bar.

In 1963 Brother Linus was teaching us the principles
of a chain reaction with billiard balls. Back then
the days were counterfeit and easy to spend.
Time was a forest of dried flowers. In 1986
it was Lorca's morning glory the woman had pinned
in her hair, a little flowering weed snatched from love's
buttonhole, and their table was filled with yellow jessamine,
white aster, bluebells, passion flowers
they must have picked themselves, all those poems
with flowers, the poems *were* flowers,
Lorca wrote once, *a garden of possibilities,*
and the words were butterflies always moving away,

walking to the park at 5:00 p.m. because, he wrote once,
that was *the hour the gardens begin to suffer.*

This late, boredom was racking up the balls.
This late it was Willie Mosconi waltzing around the table
towards another run, surrounded by headless shadows,
it was The Hustler, it was Minnesota Fats and Fast
Eddy Felsen racking them up all night, the world on hold,
taking the blue chalk in one hand, twisting fate
over the tip of the stick, setting down the chalk in
one sure motion on the table without taking your eyes
from the perfect shot taking shape on the table below you.
It was desperation in its ragged coat.
It was the decaying radium glow of the ceiling lights.
It was luck stamping its feet, the dog at the bar
not bothering to raise its head, cursing each missed shot
of our own lives, cursing the Falangists
who gunned down Lorca and buried him in a nameless field.

But that night it was chance calculating the physics for
a perfect combination shot to the side pocket.
It has been thirty years since it was first proposed
that electrons follow every possible path
through the layers of parallel universes we live in at one time.
It is true that each universe is a kind of pool pocket
we are trying to enter with one of desire's elaborate shots.
It is true that electrons tunnel from one pocket to another.
Which brings me to 1965, New York
on the steps of the same building Lorca lived in,
singing Spanish songs so badly it budged
the old men in their only clothes from the Harlem steps.
The only girl I remember kept my vase of purple flowers,
railroad vines whose tracks led beyond
the Long Island beaches where I found them
in some lovers' graveyard, the small hollow
in the dunes scattered with sticky
tissues, cigarette butts, used condoms, underwear,

and those petals strewn about that must have flowered
in someone's hair. I waited for hours trying
to glimpse into another universe. I just sat there
behind the brush while the steamers were
heading towards places with names that never seemed real.

Now we were covered with blue chalk dust looking like
big flowers, larkspurs, maybe, absurd irises,
and the old couple who never heard of García Lorca were
listening to the plaintive songs of Patsy Cline, they were
weathering whatever loneliness they feared,
they were going to dance again, to keep quarters
in the jukebox, calling yesterday back
just as she was almost out the door,
calling her back with all her friends
and their empty bottles of whatever, their jessamine,
the bluebells on the table in front of them.

I was going to play it safe on a night when nothing
had been falling for me, on a night when I took up
the stick again for the last rack, when the little second hand
on the clock hesitated between leaps. I was going to
nudge the cue ball to the far cushion then let it glance
back to the triangle of balls for this break—let someone
else make the mistakes this time, but I looked up instead
from a perfect cross corner shot, the only one
I'd make all night, and you were gone, you were disappearing
with that one lost moment of perfect grace into the rain,
and I was still facing the scattered table that didn't seem real
any longer, thinking *this is how it ends,* both of us
lost by then, but I was brushing the blue chalk off
for good, I was trying to figure which way you had gone,
trying to recall the name of that purple flower,
one universe filling the pockets of the next, Lorca gone,
time slipping off the barstool, leaving it swiveling,
the words of Lorca's general echoing through the rain,
coffee, give him plenty of coffee, by which he meant death,
the holy electrons, the lost worlds, all of them going on.

DAVID WOJAHN

Necromancy: The Last Days of Brian Jones, 1968

Hair fanning out, he'll float upside down,
Like the end, and beginning, of *Sunset Boulevard.*
Kicked out of the band, he's come home
To his manor in St. John's Wood—acid,

Hard drugs, delivered by minions to poolside,
Where for months on the nod he strums his National Steel,
Sprawled on a Day-Glo deck chair, lavender strobes
Festooning the water. He'll drown on his last meal,

Then fall to the chlorined deep end. But today he's dressed
As a wizard, star-checked robe and pointed cap,
Cover props from *His Satanic Majesty's Request.*
A syringe and phone are on his lap

But who does the necromancer call? Dial tone.
Hair fanning out, he'll float upside down.

NANCY SCHOENBERGER

Epithalamion

Let the cruel spring begin, Sweeney.
I've had too many lovers as it is,
though I think of them as husbands,
and I think of them,
but it's *me* that I remember.
As if, poised on the brink of a river,
I was part of that river. Take the Mississippi:
nearby in Murphy's Pharmacy
Van Morrison sang *brown-eyed girl*
where Manuel and I wolfed down our hamburgers.
That was Baton Rouge, and, narcissistic,
those songs were always me in my green time.

Not that all this yearn and pull is over.
Far from it: Opehlia's floating
down the Thames in her blue underthings.
Now if my lovers have married other women,
so be it: I don't care. In my best fantasy
I'm beautiful, in a rose-pink gown. It's silly,
yes, I know that—it goes on. I'm surrounded
by animals: sloe-eyed does, pigeons, cows
returned to their wild state—even giraffes—
everyone horned, hoofed, and feathered.

We form one long procession down the levee
among Exxon's refineries, like a page
out of Kipling. You're wondering what's missing

as we move along: no wedding knives,
no altar, and no one in this picture
to declare that beauty.

JIM ELLEDGE

Duckling, Swan

In bunches bright as marigolds,
azaleas, bachelor's-
buttons, women outnumber men ten to one
on this drizzling morning's commuter,
women who have big hair, chit-
chat about the week's
*Geraldo*s, glare my way as I board.

I admit it.

        In my black motorcycle jacket
I'm nothing like a god. Not
even close. In black toe to crown,
I'm more the demon dreamt than
trumpeting archangel floating
through a cumulus of Lady
Clairol creations, striding past
tips on P.C. muscle
exercises and the futures market.
Doing my best Jim Morrison,
I admit it: I love how, still glaring,
they steal peeks at my crotch.

As if it matters, I think of Terry
Herrick, the beautiful j.d. of Prather Jr.
High who grew hair before any of
us and showed off in the showers, who
curling an index finger, brought
cheerleaders to their knees,

who taught me how to inhale without
choking, who kept
Johnny Redman from kicking
my ass more times than I remember,
who pimped his mother, who was offed
by the St. Louis mob.

And then my hand touched
brings me back to the downpour, the rails
paralleling I-55, the minutes between
departure and arrival strung
out slow as a cello's moan,
to the other fiction, the one so real my
gut aches to bursting.

                    A woman
across the aisle, abandoned by her
friends for the café car,
for the little girl's, for other
acquaintances seats away, draws her hand
back, leans over the aisle, and mouths,
Can I pet your leather?

RICHARD BLESSING

Elegy for Elvis

August, 1977

Elvis lay cool in his thick shadow
and saw it was an island no one
would come to ever again. It was Memphis
and summer. It was winter. Snow was falling
blue as Christmas. It was so still
he heard his heart fill like a lonesome hotel.

Listen, John Berryman used to like to say,
Whyncha ask me whattis like to be famous?
What did he know, King? What did he know?
He never sold a million. When he died
not many women looked at their lives
like closets of spikes and pointy toes
and asked, *What good is any of it now?*

Dr. Nichopoulous was saying, *Come on, Presley,*
breathe for me, but you were happy. You'd played
your last request. Snow settled around you
like a thousand paternity suits. Ice
filled the island trees. You had gone farther
than a gossip magazine. You planned to name
your shadow for the first American to say,
I never heard of him.

Presley, you always breathed for me,
rock-bellied, up from Tupelo, a place
pastoral enough for elegy. Now one of us

is dead. Tender as Whitman's lilac sprig,
I leave these plastic flowers in the snow.
What perishes is only really real.
I twist the dial and you are everywhere.

DENNIS FINNELL

Over *Voice of America*

Some nights the quiet is all wrong. A tape,
it plays white noise. These nights I crown
myself in earphones and tune the short-wave in
to new music of the sphere. Grandmother voice
over Radio Albania wants to send over a hit
about wheat, and love. Over *Voice of America*
our voice is simply enunciated as if only
foreigners have ears. Silence is a drawn chord.
Between Tirane and Washington the static is
a Geiger counter gone sane. I tune the BBC.
The Repulsive Aliens play their catchy music—
codas from the white dwarf before collapse.

Some evenings I haunt my office. Windows open
out to Mary Lyon's grave and campus maples
kept pretty by will. The hour we love between
dog and wolf comes as stars show up, up there
all along. In my dark office I drink coffee
I cannot see, start to disappear. I make up
faces for students blasting maples and her grave
with Culture Club, The Police. Hair is green,
cheeks flower white. Mary Lyon said, "Testify!"
Dickinson took a carriage over the Holyoke Range
to her own seminary of despair, a dress
kept white in legend and a whiter sustenance.

More white than crystals Parker melted in spoons,
a hero addicted to pain. Students here know

Stalin's white Siberia and each red cent doctors
earn in their cures. They know Reggie Jackson,
Patton. Bird is black, fiendish, jazz-like.
Modifiers are right and wrong. Bird did burn
his room in a colored L.A. hotel, yelled Fire,
colored and naked. He did die in a baroness'
Manhattan suite, laughing at Dorsey on TV.
Don't those stories kill? From L.A. to New York,
from fire to laughter, he played hopeless rooms
we can inhabit because he did not need hope.

Bird lived, died, lives some more. The last time
I visited Dickinson's grave, it was occupied.
Inside the black iron fence young lovers lay
clothed on her grave. He was on her and on her.
I have not yet been back. Friends, make sense
of those lovers. Were they mocking the virgin
in legend, she who knew Babylon inside out?
Tell me in some nights a Parker solo hums
also out of you, or a Dickinson phrase
moves your lips, cryptically. Our ears record
sounds of dead stars. Tell me we call them back
since they call us and we can hear, once again.

DAN SICOLI

"All Shook Up"

in there these short hairs
pumped up parodying
the king
swinging axes as if
they once could hack
at a melody
screaming
"i'm on drugs. . . . i'm all
fucked up!"
and below these
dressupforeachothermommy suburbanites
slam dance to it all at center stage

spiked pinned dyed ripped
pseudo-neo-punks pretend life is a war
in packs they worship
little gods
suicide is still an alien virgin

if you're serious
become the night
lick dry heels of fallen winoes
abandon weapons
let wounds bleed freely
shave head with dull razor
eat public trash
sleep in cracked concrete cunt womb soul darkness
vomit at every opportunity

spit on doctor preacher police politician
train eyes to be frozen dead cat
french kiss anus of city
wake with it on your breath
call yourself nigger one
and exhale

and when you begin
to lust the ultimate
start counting backwards
from 10. . . .

ALISON STONE

Rocket to Russia

I woke up with purple hair and Paul
Beside me, grinning as he tried to
Put a blue stripe on Jenni.
She rolled over, stained
The pillowcase. My contact lenses
Felt like glass, my mouth tasted like I was chewing
On a sock. I had to get to school. We were doing
One of the important wars.

Walking to the subway in the rain I cursed my mom
For lending me her pointy boots. Jenni and I
Discussed Shakespeare and mescaline, and why
Our boyfriends preferred men. On the train
A woman asked if I'd been
Mugged. Krazy Kolor had run down my forehead
And become a wound.

D O R O T H Y   B A R R E S I

Venice Beach: Brief Song

Maybe Zizi is right.
Rocket a mile up, look back,

and we're all just earthlings in restaurants
talking low, trying to figure

one thing out, or
stop one thing from happening.

And all the crystal meth in the world
cannot lift even one of our bodies

free of this argument, or set us clear
of the boardwalk's great

stake in pleasure. Still
the hypodermic shadow of the Capitol Records Building

is oddly comforting,
and the Sufi on rollerskates

promises the next tune is ours
on a boom box he's hoisted

like huge hope to his many-robed shoulder:
Bix Beiderbecke and the boys,

"I'm Coming Virginia."
This is not the life we requisitioned for.

But what can we do now that we're here?
When Larry leaves, when Frances

makes her final point and leaves,
and Zizi never showed (she had something to frame),

I know what I'll do.
Contrive a window like this one

where I'll lean out in the old, theatrical
self-wounding way—oh the buoy bells

of loneliness! Oh the black
candles under waves!—but still

tasting cooler air on my face
like a fire hydrant blowing.

Like a different promise.
Then I'll bless the heads of the insane skateboarders,

those little dooms in their
acid-orange knee pads.

Last night they kept me awake
with their breakneck wheels, their passion. Tonight

I'll watch them marry the pit
city fathers laid years ago, and imagining that

gesture of local
wisdom or submission

will be like imagining this prayer for a change:
to be truly blonde, and just once

blown away, flying and flying and flying.

TAD RICHARDS

A Challenge to the Reader

At this point, Ellery
Queen is possessed
Of all the clues he needs to bring the case
To a fitting conclusion.

Nothing has been hidden.
Using only
What you have learned already, Dear Reader,
Can you unmask the culprit?

Chapter X: You're Probably Wondering Why I Called You All Here

I do not think you will
Ever have to
Make a decision, but you will. There must
Always be a last chapter,

The detective must stand
By the fireplace,
Tapping his cigar ash, and explaining
How he came to understand

How it all happened,
Even in real life,
Where one murder blends into another,
And even the private eye

Posing by the fireplace,
Wine glass in hand,
May find his coattails aflame, and the chase
Begun all over again.

Chapter XI: A Possible Break in the Case

Tall (not as tall as I),
Soft-spoken,
Even sullen, he appears more transparent
Than perhaps he is; meanwhile,

He lurks in the foreground.
He may well be
The suspect we've been seeking all along.
But what about motive?

Chapter XII: The Clue Pursued

I've never seen Paul drink
At the Homestead.
When I'm there, he walks in, glares balefully,
And walks right back out again.

Once we did speak words, though,
A chance meeting.
I said, "Two dollars worth of regular,
Please," and he just said, "OK."

I wanted to say more,
Put him at ease,
But there was hardly time, and what business
Was it of mine to put him

At ease? When it was months
Before I could
Even bring myself to think of him by
Name, although I knew his name.

But I would have: if he'd
Grunted at me,
"Say, aren't you . . . ?" I'd have owned up, and told him,
"Sure, and I know who you are,

But don't be concerned, I
Have no substance
As far as she's concerned—I can't steal her,
Although I would if I could."

Chapter XIII: Interlude

Sherlock Holmes and Sam Spade
Got nothin', child,
On me; Sergeant Friday, Charlie Chan, and
Boston Blackie. No matter

Where she's hidin', she's gon'
See me comin'—
Gonna walk right down that street like Bull Dog
Drummond, I'm gonna find her. . . .

Chapter XIV: Conclusion

I would be the other
Suspect, sought for
Conspiracy to entertain your soul,
The one who's too obvious,

And therefore easily
Relegated
To the status of colorful minor
Character, memorable

But not central. I can
Go along with
That—I'm memorable but not central
To myself, for that matter,

But it hasn't quite seemed to
Work out, has it?
I've been written out a couple of times,
My alibi has been cleared,

I've been told I could go
Home, all charges
Have been dropped—but each time, even without
New evidence coming to light,

I keep reappearing.
What's to be done?
Remember, you have all the clues you need
To solve this thing—or I might,

In a dramatic plot
Reversal, be
Bumped off and dumped in an alley, but that
Would be another story.

Bryan Ferry

And as the world turns, so turns the light:
Monet, for twenty years, paints at his lilies—
The subject, truly, light: yet it has weight.
The cool, ironic reds, rebellious yellows—
The bitter, blue-tinged ridge of green that shelves
Upon a deep mauve sky, upon the eye,
Bend with the form and flesh of things themselves.
In surface light there lies eternity.

Your voice, once half in love with novelty,
Now paints at the lonely heart, and though its moods
May move so slowly only the tireless eye
May see, you see. It lies like water weeds,
Always though never the same. You clear your throat—
And as the heart turns, so turns the light.

KEVIN STEIN

World without End

Before my brother-in-law lost his telephone job
   to the first recession
a brief war wouldn't cure, he worked alone
   200 feet beneath
the humped-back hills of Southern Indiana,

tending AT&T fiber optics, and as unexpected bonus,
   two obsolete coaxial cables
linking both coasts to some hard rock Colorado
   mountain sanctuary,
where blips adorn a panoply of mint green screens

and everyone wears headphones, though the jamming
   they listen to
isn't music to anyone's ears. Among clay and the muzzles
   of brown spotted cattle,
his site was bomb proofed—replete with freeze dried stew,

bottled water, backup diesel generators and a score
   of acid batteries
to back up those, and shiny silver suits with gloves
   supple enough
to squeeze an M-16's trigger on the irradiated masses.

"A link in the Armageddon line," he called it,
   brutal with humor,
and don't start now with your moral imperatives.
   It was work,
twenty-three years better than Arkansas share cropping

that broke his parents, even their mules too sway backed
	to auction off,
and who could feed two hay-hungry pets? Before he shot
	those mules,
he took the instamatic photograph he's taped to his

grey metal desk, underground, 194 feet deeper than where
	they lay.
It's the photo we go retrieve, his last day, a bit drunk,
	rain emptying the sky
as if it had no intention of stopping there: soon

the ozone-depleted atmosphere, next the moon, perhaps
	a skein of stars
who'd corroborate the luckless Chicken Little, and then
	the sun itself,
shrunken into the pin prick of borrowed light

his miner's cap pokes through elevator dark. Slow,
	chilled ride.
We lower as if hand over hand into the room's incessant,
	denture-like clacking:
each raised receiver, each dial tone, each good-bye, so long,

click. "Yes, I'll wear my black dress, black pumps
	and sequined shawl."
"Have you heard about . . . ," "and mother always . . . ,"
	"No, I said. No."
How do I explain my urge to listen, my appetite for love

and anger that's not mine? Or worse, my yearning to pull
	the plug,
prompt the plural shaking of heads in hallways and kitchens,
	a plangent chorus
of "Hello, hello? . . ."—or safe below a rock shelf

the first anxious "We've lost them, sir," the scurrying
	and alarms,
a dream of missiles like rain from purple clouds, and then

[226]

that haunted cloud,
the shape of fear sauteed in a pan of ignorance,

served with lunch. But the cold war's over,
   and thankfully
my brother-in-law has switched on the radio he wired
   down the shaft,
against all company regulations. It's tuned to oldies,

and I half-expect Sha Na Na's obnoxious "Get a Job,"
   for irony's sake.
It's Van Morrison, instead, his group Them doing
   the original version
of "Gloria," Van punctuating the "i" with fists in the gut.

We dance, play air guitar, both of us blue-haloed
   by banks of lights
installed to counter Seasonal Affective Disorder.
   Who could be sad,
dear reader, in such a state of grace? Buried in earth,

a grand reconciliation taking place around us,
   entombed with music—
if not of the spheres—then of voices speaking,
   listeners listening,
and hope, our sturdy friend, solid as two good mules.

LYNDA HULL

Night Waitress

Reflected in the plate glass, the pies
look like clouds drifting off my shoulder.
I'm telling myself my face has character,
not beauty. It's my mother's Slavic face.
She washed the floor on hands and knees
below the Black Madonna, praying
to her god of sorrows and visions
who's not here tonight when I lay out the plates,
small planets, the cups and moons of saucers.
At this hour the men all look
as if they'd never had mothers.
They do not see me. I bring the cups.
I bring the silver. There's the man
who leans over the jukebox nightly
pressing the combinations
of numbers. I would not stop him
if he touched me, but it's only songs
of risky love he leans into. The cook sings
with the jukebox, a moan and sizzle
into the grill. On his forehead
a tattooed cross furrows,
diminished when he frowns. He sings words
dragged up from the bottom of his lungs.
I want a song that rolls
through the night like a big Cadillac
past factories to the refineries
squatting on the bay, round and shiny

as the coffee urn warming my palm.
Sometimes when coffee cruises my mind
visiting the most remote way stations,
I think of my room as a calm arrival
each book and lamp in its place. The calendar
on my wall predicts no disaster
only another white square waiting
to be filled like the desire that fills
jail cells, the old arrest
that makes me stare out the window or want
to try every bar down the street.
When I walk out of here in the morning
my mouth is bitter with sleeplessness.
Men surge to the factories and I'm too tired
to look. Fingers grip lunch box handles,
belt buckles gleam, wind riffles my uniform
and it's not romantic when the sun unlids
the end of the avenue. I'm fading
in the morning's insinuations
collecting in the crevices of buildings,
in wrinkles, in every fault
of this frail machinery.

JOYCE CAROL OATES

Waiting on Elvis, 1956

This place up in Charlotte called Chuck's where I
used to waitress and who came in one night
but Elvis and some of his friends before his concert
at the Arena, I was twenty-six married but still
waiting tables and we got to joking around like you
do, and he was fingering the lace edge of my slip
where it showed below my hemline and I hadn't even
seen it and I slapped at him a little saying, You
sure are the one aren't you feeling my face burn but
he was the kind of boy even meanness turned sweet in
his mouth.

Smiled at me and said, Yeah honey I guess I sure am.

JUDITH VOLLMER

Wildsisters Bar

After Friedan & the flare
of Millett, the rebirth
of the presses & clinics,
after the Seneca Encampment,
after Kirkpatrick & Thatcher,
after welfare women remain unrescued,
I go to bed wondering why
we'll try to build a *women's space*
in the middle of a depression,
the grand notions of our art
boiling & simmering on a stove
with one working burner.

How do you operate a jackhammer if
you've never owned a toolbox?
Who knows how to vent a stinking drain?
Those questions and the pleasing ones—
can we invite the Roches
to do a gig soon?—
pound at us while we build fire walls, sand chairs, replace wiring.
The unemployed guitarist who lives upstairs
solemnly agrees that Neil Young is the father of punk.
We move on to Grace Jones,
Grace Slick. May the mother of punk
be with us forever,
her fierce & beautiful curls
forever in our faces.
Neighborhood men drop by the hundred-year-old

building while we work, give us the raised fist.
How's the *sisterhood* going? Slowly. According
to Rita, who hasn't seen a paycheck in 90 days
and works this project between bus trips
to the welfare line, the work is moving.

*

The trauma nurse wheels Rita into surgery for the fifth time. No
   one
is saying why was she out so late and why was she out so late
in a place like that. Because her swollen body, filled with the
   yellow
sap of infection, is something even we don't recognize.

*

If I could I'd call de Beauvoir or Leduc and say
things haven't changed much.
Store windows fill up
with plastic women-corpses,
mouths pursed in false horror,
legs parted as if dreading that which
in breathless joy
might open them further.
Histrionics in the Foodland announces
Joan of Arc kidney beans & Aunt Jemima's daughter
for the Eighties.
The only women on MTV
are half-dressed & half-witted.
We want art
for those on the brink
of finding a place to speak,
who want
desire
that short-
circuits the voice box.

*

Only the hum of the ice machine
and the quiet bubble of soup,
Lee's hair turning to silk
under the bar lights.
On this, the night before opening
I'm happy as the girl who
turned back her bed covers and found
nothing but roses,
happy as I dream of Dana
lost in a tub of bubbles and herbs
after long days and no time
for bathing
or sweet sleep.
Happy we're all on fine tuning
waiting for the slow pulse of music,
the clink & glisten of glasses,
the faces shining at the door.

                    *

Rita, returned from death with one strong leg,
my friends in your patience & wit,
here are tools we need:
two, or six voices in agreement, encouragement
when one voice hears no answer;
the heavy bucket of nails
the neighborhood men left by the door for us,
the kettle boiling its resistance in the 50-degree room,
simple things, some large, though,   .
like loneliness,
like the grip of a hand saying good-bye,
the face greeting us at the door
falling off its hinges.

JUDSON MITCHAM

On the Otis Redding Bridge

Macon, Georgia

This morning, when a woman walks home
from the graveyard shift at the cotton mill;
when she comes to the Otis Redding Bridge, coughing,

and turning her head, so the snowflake dust
on her shirt whirls off through a sheer gold sleeve
the early sun lays across the road,

                                  I want to sing
with the voice of Otis Redding—

with the power that would let a man shout
sanctified, tender, and sad, let him cry,
angry, yet shocking in his praise.

                                   I want to sing
the cotton dust caught in the sunlight;
and the woman who is not slowed down in the least
by the momentary beauty that began

as an old pain deep in her lungs; this woman
who spits off the bridge and goes on.

Contributors' Notes and Comments

PETER BALAKIAN is the author of three books of poems, most recently *Reply from Wilderness Island,* and of *Theodore Roethke's Far Fields.* He edits, with Bruce Smith, the *Graham House Review* and is Professor of English at Colgate.

"At its best, rock and roll has something to do with what Federico García Lorca calls *duende*: 'pure music with a body so lean it could stay in the air . . . that stormy ocean of love freed from Time . . . which burns the blood like a poultice of broken glass.' In its totality, American rock might be viewed as one long, never-to-be-finished American epic poem. A rock song could be like a light of revelation, and it held the script of where you were and how you were feeling. In this poem, a young teenager is talking to his girlfriend on the phone after midnight. The objects of the house are transformed. There's yearning within and freedom out there. And the music yokes the two."

DOROTHY BARRESI's *All of the Above* won the 1990 Barnard New Women Poets Prize. Her poems have appeared in many literary journals, including *Poetry, Ploughshares,* the *Denver Quarterly,* and the *Indiana Review.* She teaches creative writing and contemporary literature at California State University/Northridge.

"Everything in my life has had a rock chord as its countermelody: I grew up listening, as though my life depended on it, to the Stones, the Clash, Dylan, a hundred and one punk bands with names like Hammer Damage, Baloney-Heads, the Bizarros, the Rubber City Rebels, and then Springsteen and the 'college' bands like R.E.M. and U2. If the urgency and machine-gun music of rock has infiltrated my poetry, and I hope it has, then it has happened by osmosis. I'm still listening."

CHARLES BAXTER, author of four books of fiction and a book of poetry, *Imaginary Paintings*, teaches at the University of Michigan and lives in Ann Arbor.

"What is reported in 'The Purest Rage' is very close to what I saw and heard at an Ann Arbor intersection. Against the loud and exuberant expansiveness of the music, I saw this enclosed couple silently (to me) experiencing their unhappiness. For me, the poetry of the situation was in the meeting of rock and roll and silent, private, rage."

BRUCE BERGER's collection of desert essays, *The Telling Distance*, won the 1990 Western States Book Award for Creative Nonfiction and the 1991 Colorado Book Authors Award. His poems appear in *Poetry* and *New Letters*.

"'Salad Days' refers to the relationship between the pianist and the drummer—myself and my friend Luis, respectively—in the following bands: Starfis, in Puerto de Santa Maria, 1965; Simbroni, in Altea, 1966; and Los Everplay, in Torremolinos, 1967. The towns are all in southern Spain."

JUDITH BERKE's first book, *White Morning*, was followed by her chapbook, *Acting Problems*. She is completing a second, book-length collection, *Not Eden*.

RICHARD BLESSING's books are *A Closed Book, A Passing Season, Poems and Stories*, and *Winter Constellations*.

DAVID BOTTOMS's first book, *Shooting Rats at the Bibb County Dump*, was chosen by Robert Penn Warren as winner of the 1979 Walt Whitman Award of the Academy of American Poets. His poems have appeared widely in magazines such as the *Atlantic*, the *New Yorker*, *Harper's*, *Poetry*, and the *Paris Review*, as well as in numerous anthologies and textbooks. Bottoms is the author of two other books of poems, *In a U-Haul North of Damascus* and *Under the Vulture-Tree*, as well as two novels, *Any Cold Jordan* and *Easter Weekend*. Among his other awards are the Levinson Prize, an Ingram Merrill Award, and an Award in Literature from the American Academy and Institute of Arts and Letters.

"Lester Flatt probably wouldn't care much for the musical company he finds in this anthology, and he belongs here only for the influence he exerted on early rock and roll musicians. He was a traditionalist and a purist, and he represents the epitome of the mountain voice of the southern Appalachians. His long career was dedicated to the preservation of authentic American folk music. This wasn't always easy. There were temptations to commercialize—from Hollywood, from New York record companies, and from his own partner, Earl Scruggs, who in the last years of their relationship grew more and more interested in bending their sound toward contemporary folk and rock music. All of this contributed to the breakup of the Foggy Mountain Boys, the finest band in the history of bluegrass music. But Flatt remained true to his vision. He formed the Nashville Grass and went on with his music."

NEAL BOWERS is the author of three poetry collections, the most recent *Night Vision*, and two critical studies. His poems have appeared in *Harper's*, the *New Yorker*, *Poetry*, the *Sewanee Review*, *Shenandoah*, and many other journals. He teaches at Iowa State University and edits *Poet & Critic*.

"Rock and roll (the pre-1970 variety) connects point A to point B. It gets me from home to work and back again, the cassette player making a blur of the miles. Sometimes, I sing along and forget for a beat or two that it's not 1965. Like Cary Grant in *Notorious*, it has the power to save us from the poisonous present. Oh, Elvis transcendent, inscribe my name!"

VAN K. BROCK, Editor-in-Chief of *International Quarterly*, teaches in the Writing Program at Florida State University. His poems have been included in numerous anthologies, among them *Strong Measures: Contemporary American Poetry in Traditional Forms*, and a collection of poems, *The Hard Essential Landscape*, is in the Contemporary Poetry Series, University Presses of Florida. His essay "Images of Elvis, the South, and America" appears in *Elvis: Images and Fancies*.

"After Elvis's death, I became interested in the intricate intertwining of Elvis as a myth, the media phenomenon and the cultures in America and abroad that, with his music and performance genius, created the myth. 'Mary's Dream' is adapted from an account told to me by Mary, a woman from New York whom I met at Graceland a year after Elvis's death, and 'Sphinx' arises out of the study and experience of Elvis, his life, and America."

SIDNEY BURRIS has published a collection of his poems, *A Day at the Races*. He has also produced a volume on the poetry of Seamus Heaney, and a number of his essays and poems have appeared in *Poetry*, the *Atlantic*, the *Southern Review*, the *Sewanee Review*, and the *Virginia Quarterly Review*. He is at work on a new collection of poetry, a book on W. H. Auden, and a collection of literary essays.

"It is very difficult, if not impossible, for me to perform any sort of autobiographical excavation without one of these songs or musicians turning up. The question, of course, becomes one of incorporating this rambunctious material into the orderly confines of verse. I have chosen to view this music, yet once more—who hasn't?—as deeply cultural and to allow the context in which the music appears to supply the presiding judgment."

KELLY CHERRY's twelve books include *My Life and Dr. Joyce Brothers*, a novel in stories; *The Exiled Heart*, an inquiry into the nature of meaning; *God's Loud Hand*, her newest collection of poetry; and a translation of the *Octavia* of Seneca. In 1989 she received the first Fellowship of Southern Writers Poetry Award (the Hanes Prize) in recognition of a body of work.

"I was never any good at pop culture, but that doesn't mean I didn't try to be. There was a tavern at the end of the road, and after school let out and before dinner, high school kids were allowed in to dance. The rumor was that, if a scout spotted you, you would get to be on the Dick Clark show. You would be on television, a thought that thrilled me although I had never seen a television except in newspaper advertisements. I had a circle skirt—two circle skirts. One was made of felt; the other was a blue-and-white dotted Swiss that I had made myself in Home Ec, sewing the heart-shaped pocket by hand. I wore a white sleeveless blouse with a V-neck. Under my circle skirt I had crinolines, stiff and flirty. But all this sophistication was nothing compared with the black-and-white saddle shoes and rolled white socks.

"My sister, younger by two-and-a-half years, observed my shenanigans on the dance floor with disapproval. On the way home she said, 'I was so embarrassed! I was so ashamed! You're not supposed to move your hips like that when you dance!'

"I tried a very few more times in my life to learn to dance. The bop, the twist, the two-step. I never got the hang of any of them. Besides, when I was seventeen, a sophomore at the New Mexico Institute of Mining and Technology, a guy who had actually said he loved me hauled off and slapped me on a dance floor. He was twenty-four, a graduate student in physics. I can't remember what it was I had done wrong. Maybe it didn't have anything to do with dancing.

"My course load that semester included calculus, physics, analytic geometry, anthropology, mechanical drawing, something else I've forgotten. On my own, I read *Doctor Zhivago*, a dry, piney wind sweeping sand through the dormitory, which resembled a bunker. Home was far away; my parents said it would be silly—a waste of money—to go back for Thanksgiving or even Christmas. Did my parents ever write, telephone? On my birthday, I did calculus problems from seven in the morning until ten at night. (Those are the exact hours. I wanted to see if I could keep doing problems without stopping.) Some nights I went walking by myself in the gulch, the moon as bright as a flashlight. I didn't go to any more dances.

"There were car rides, though, flying fast over long stretches of deserted southern highway. For a semester.

"After that I adopted a bystander's relation to pop culture. For a while, there were Janis Joplin, the Grateful Dead, the Jefferson Airplane. Microminis superseded by maxicoats superseded by power suits. Fishnet stockings followed by thigh-high kickass boots followed by pumps-for-professionals followed by Nikes. (I await the return of saddle shoes.) Fashion is everywhere. What is the pop culture of American politics but fashion? What is the pop culture of contemporary fiction but fashion? In time, a woman settles down. She lives alone. No one asks her to dance, but an American woman, even a bystander, even a wallflower, lives in a pop world. Fashion *is* everywhere. Lately, lately, I pop—pop!—popcorn and watch the Academy Awards on television. I read *People* Magazine. I even read *Vanity Fair*, which is top-of-the-pop pop, pure promo, la crème de la puff.

"And sometimes I remember what it was like, riding in a car, the windows down, the radio on. . . .

"I don't think my sister remembers what she said. I would never bring it up to her. She could never have guessed that I would be foolish enough to take her childish words so seriously. . . .

"To be loved, I think, would be like being included, made a part of that chic clique, the human race. Women are always promising to be true. If a woman were loved in return, I think, she would feel like she was in an automobile, riding along, with somebody beside her because that's where he wanted to be. She would be tapping her foot in time to the beat. She would be dancing to the beat of her heart."

JUDITH ORTIZ COFER's poetry has appeared in numerous journals, including the *Georgia, Antioch, Kenyon,* and *Southern* reviews and in her two collections, *Terms of Survival* and *Reaching for the Mainland.* Her volume of poetry and prose *The Latin Deli* is forthcoming.

"The Stones' song is mentioned in a poem about living in the moment—music is a key element in the impulse."

MARK DEFOE recently published a chapbook of his poetry, *Palmate.*

"Both of these poems came floating back to me, a sort of rock and roll nostalgia. They speak of a group memory, too, of the fifties and sixties. Rock music was in the texture of these times—in the shrieking chaos of a fire fight in Nam, in the earnest chanting for justice and flower power, in slow dancing with your one-and-only in the gym, in groping hot flesh at the passion pit, in kicking down Main with absolutely nothing to do. Who knows what was real? It is all memory, caught forever in a rock tune, a blues lyric, a protest song, a guitar riff. It's just a rock and roll dream, but, of course, never forgettable."

RITA DOVE's many books include *Fifth Sunday, Museum, Thomas and Beulah,* and *The Yellow House on the Corner.* Her latest works include a book of poetry, *Grace Notes,* and *Through the Ivory Gate,* a novel. She has won a Pulitzer Prize for her poetry. She is Commonwealth Professor of English at the University of Virginia.

JIM ELLEDGE has published two collections of poetry, *Nothing Nice* and *Various Envies.* His poems have appeared in the *Paris Review,* the *North American Review,* the *Denver Quarterly,* the *Antioch Review, Poet & Critic,* and the *Texas Review,* as well as in many other journals. He teaches at Illinois State University and edits the *Illinois Review.*

"During my junior year in high school, I was fortunate to have taken a course in U.S. history—World War II to the present—taught by Hilda Smith, the only thought-provoking teacher I ever had at Granite City Senior High. She covered the expected historical events, of course, but also, near the end of that spring semester, brought us up-to-date on current events, particularly Civil Rights and the Vietnam Conflict. She offered documents. She gave statistics. She raised questions—but never expected easy answers. Ms. Smith also brought in some recordings by 'protest singers,' in particular Joan Baez and Bob Dylan.

"The Beatles had been on the charts for several years by then: 'I Wanna Hold Your Hand,' 'She Loves You,' 'Twist and Shout,' etc.— the fluff stuff. Like so many of my generation, I was a fan, but when I heard Dylan for the first time, I realized the Beatles' 'Yeah, yeah, yeah' was about as inane as pop lyrics could get. When Dylan sang, 'It's a hard rain's a-gonna fall' or 'The answer is blowin' in the wind,' I was engaged in ways I'd never been before.

"I didn't know the songs by Dylan that Ms. Smith played for us that day were already 'old' nor that Dylan had switched genres, from folk to rock, as he would do time and time again during his career. Expecting songs which protested the injustices rampant in our society, I bought Dylan's *Highway 61 Revisited*, the only LP by him I could find, and put it on my hi-fi. I was amazed, to say the least. The album was like nothing I'd ever heard. The music was more riveting than anything I'd heard on the radio or bought in record shops—perhaps not *great* rock and roll but *different* in a way even now I'm unable to explain. But, for me, the real difference lay not in the music but in the lyrics. For the first time in my life, I was presented with metaphor that intrigued me, sparked my imagination, spoke to me—although often I had no idea what it said.

"I became more than a fan. I became a devotee. I hunted down and bought everything by Bob Dylan I could find, not just his rock and roll but the earlier, folk LPs, too. I also read everything about him I could find. There wasn't much, an article here and there, a poorly written biography.

"I'd been writing what I thought of then as poetry for a few years, something part Hallmark card verse and part teenage angst. I'd read somewhere that Dylan had admired the poet Dylan Thomas so much that he'd changed his name as a sort of homage, and I decided I should read something by the poet. Oddly, my high-school library had a copy of Thomas's *Collected Poems*. In it I found what I'd discovered in the lyricist's songs—metaphor that fascinated me although, again, I was at a loss to interpret it. But interpretation had nothing to do with my enjoyment of either artist's work—not for me, not in those days, not even now, really. For me, the importance was how the language—in Dylan's lyrics, in Thomas's poems—addressed me in ways I couldn't articulate, how it addressed what I was experiencing.

"I listened to Dylan more than I read Thomas, and from the singer, I learned the importance of scene for setting a mood; of image, metaphor, and simile for revealing, not telling, emotion; of building a whole based on its parts; of moving within the work from point A to point Z—and no doubt much more.

"The instruction I first had regarding the craft of poetry didn't come from any of the 'masters' of poetry, but from Bob Dylan; not from an English teacher (in fact, I was not 'permitted' to sign up for the creative writing class the then-head of our high-school English department taught on an invitation-only basis) but from a history teacher.

"We all know, at least metaphorically, where Dylan is now. I have no idea what happened to Ms. Smith, who left Granite City Senior High at the end of that semester. Rumor had it that she'd been fired for being a Communist, and given the paranoia of those Cold War days and of that lily-white, Bible-belt terrain, I wouldn't be at all surprised if that's exactly what had happened. Regardless, I owe her an inestimable debt and hope she's lived long and prospered."

DENNIS FINNELL's *Red Cottage* won the 1990 Juniper Prize from the University of Massachusetts Press. He has taught at the University of Tennessee and at Mount Holyoke College and now works mostly as a freelance writer.

"'Over *Voice of America*' was written as part of a series of letter-poems with David Graham. Each was a kind of solo, inspired partly by the letter-poem the other had written and sent. I do remember having in mind a couple of musical ideas for this poem. One was the form of the twelve-bar blues, and I used the twelve-line stanzas as 'bars,' and I tried emulating the AABA form of rhythm and blues and jazz and rock and roll, giving the poem four stanzas. I think the poem partly has to do with how a wide range of people's heroes—Charlie Parker, Emily Dickinson, the Police, the Repulsive Aliens, among others—inform people, so they are attuned to hearing things unheard before."

RICHARD FOERSTER, awarded the "Discovery"/*The Nation* Prize in 1985, is the author of *Sudden Harbor* and two chapbooks, *Transfigured Nights* and *The Hours*. He lives in York Beach, Maine, where he works as a freelance educational writer and as Associate Editor of *Chelsea*.

"The impetus behind 'Playland,' which I wrote in 1987, was the line from the Beatles' *Sgt. Pepper* album: 'It was twenty years ago today / Sgt. Pepper taught the band to play.' And so it was. I began thinking back to those seemingly liberated but awkward days of 1967. I was a senior at Fordham Prep, was dating a girl named Cathy McCloskey, and would zip about Westchester and the Bronx with her in my year-old Volkswagen Fastback (which I eventually rolled over and totaled). I had installed one of those now obsolete eight-track tapeplayers under the dash and—with all the excess of youth—wired six speakers into the roof and door panels of that tiny car. *Sgt. Pepper* was my favorite album that year, and of course the music couldn't be loud enough. I knew all the lyrics by heart. More than Eliot or Auden—or Simon and Garfunkel, those special favorites of my theology teachers—the Beatles' songs were the poetry that spoke most directly to my adolescent soul in 1967. But in 1987, another line kept going through my head: "Sgt. Pepper's lonely. Sgt. Pepper's lonely." And then that scene at Rye Playland, of necking at night alongside Long Island Sound, came back to me—and for better or worse, the significance of those fish."

ROBERT GIBB recently published a third collection of poetry, *Fugue for a Late Snow*.

"The Butterfield elegy is about a Chicago blues musician; the Russell Barron piece celebrates fifties rhythm-and-blues music. Both genres are, I think, sources upon which rock and roll draws, or did, before it became simply another commodity."

CHRISTOPHER GILBERT's first book of poetry, *Across the Mutual Landscape*, won the 1983 Walt Whitman Award; his second is *Demos/Music of the Striving That Was There*. He teaches psychology, works part-time as a psychotherapist, and plays alto sax and flute.

"'Time with Stevie Wonder in It' is both a reminiscence and a bridge into the future. The poem is claiming this about the music. It took me several years to work this poem out—from the moment when I first heard Stevie Wonder's song 'Superstition' on the radio in the early 1970s (a song which seemed to reconnect him to the beliefs and hopeful mysteries alluded to in the poem) to a moment about five years later when I was dancing to one of his synthesizer wrung dance riffs. My feeling in this poem alternates between several polarities, among them memories and anticipations, despair and hope, uselessness and beauty. The line flow and the hesitations create time for me. But what I was aiming for was music—doggone it!!! But there is one line in the poem where I really let go: 'Ray Charles, Charles Brown, Ruth Brown, Muddy and Wolf.' This is the Black American part of rock and roll. This part rolls.

"'Chosen to Be Water' is clotted with a wish for transformation, and a wish for cleansing. It is an elegy for Bob Marley, whose music united the purging side of music with the purging side of politics.

"One of the stories 'Enclosure' is about is the blues as the union of the Earth side of us and the Spirit side of us, and these two make plain ole sex—if it is ever plain. The blues embodies sex, so much so that sometimes it is a transcendent thing. This poem remembers Howlin' Wolf, who cast himself as a bad-assed sexual thing."

DANA GIOIA's poems have been collected in *Daily Horoscope*. He has edited *New Italian Poetry* and, with William J. Smith, *Poems from Italy*.

ALBERT GOLDBARTH, Distinguished Professor of Humanities at Wichita State University, is the author of numerous collections of poetry, including *Heaven and Earth*, which received the National Book Critics Circle Award, and, most recently, *The Gods*. He has also published two volumes of literary essays.

"The poem 'People Are Dropping Out of Our Lives' must be—what? twenty-one, twenty-two years old now. In a sense, the wide-eyed, poetry-drunk young man who wrote it is a stranger to me—has dropped out of my life as surely as anyone else in the poem, and takes his place for me, with all of his fiery hopes and his flaws, on a tapestry that includes the legendary figures mentioned in the poem. I suppose that's a function of rock and roll: it allows us to take our own two-bit loves and pains, our lowdown nittygritty beckonings, and our upward-yearning aspirations, and mythologize them: transform them, into the beat that's larger than we are. Whoever wrote this little poem,

I feel so distant from him, and yet so especially tender toward him. . . . He must be subsumed into the tapestry now, winning his honors there, battling his monsters."

DAVID GRAHAM has published four collections of poetry, most recently *Doggedness* and *Second Wind*. He is an AWP Award winner. The first rock concert he attended was by the Who, in 1971 at Saratoga, New York. Since 1987, he's taught English at Ripon College.

"I'm interested to note that, although my book *Second Wind* contains a section of poems devoted to music, neither of the poems selected for *Sweet Nothings* appears there. 'Jesus Never Sleeps' appears in another section of love poems, and 'Father of the Man' I placed with poems that map my travels through time and space. As is probably true of most Baby Boomers, rock and roll is simply an integral part of my life, influencing much of what I do and think, while providing metaphors for what I write.

"In a sense my poems speak to two very different aspects of rock's pervasive influence upon me and the culture at large. 'Jesus Never Sleeps' takes note of the fact that as rock and roll enters middle age, it can and has been co-opted for all sorts of salesmanship—hustling everything from soda and sneakers to the Lord. 'Father of the Man,' in contrast, asserts that rock's rebelliousness will never enter middle age. In essence, rock remains as young as ever, while those of us who grew up on it do not.

"But, as I say, I hadn't thought of these poems as being *about* rock at all. One is a love poem to the woman who attended my first rock concert with me, and the other is a sympathetic nod to my friends whose kids have entered the age when all adulthood seems pathetic."

THOM GUNN, born in England in 1929, moved to California in 1954, where he has lived ever since.

"The relation between the Elvis and Sex Pistols poems to rock and roll is obvious."

JAMES HARMS, born in 1960 in Pasadena, California, has had poems published in *Poetry*, the *American Poetry Review*, the *Kenyon Review*, *Poetry East*, *Ploughshares*, and elsewhere. His first book is *Modern Ocean*. He teaches at East Stroudsburg University in Pennsylvania.

"The title of 'When You Wish upon a Star That Turns into a Plane' is a line in the song 'Valentine' by the Replacements. The poem itself is a dramatic monologue; the speaker has the voice and perspective of a rock and roll runaway, someone who's run toward a dream and away from a comfortable, ordinary existence (in this case the ordinary is represented by the suburbs of Los Angeles). Since the speaker is on a bus bench in Hollywood, the physical distance from his/her home is short; it's the emotional and psychic distance that seems, suddenly, overwhelming. In this context, the title says it all."

LYNDA HULL, author of two books, *Ghost Money* and *Star Ledger*, has received numerous grants and awards, among them the Juniper Prize, the Edwin Piper Poetry Prize, the Carl Sandburg Award, Pushcart prizes, and a fellowship from the NEA. She teaches in the Vermont College MFA Program.

"Both of these poems grew out of the atmosphere of Newark's bluesy, gritty exhaustion, its anger and soulfulness, the powerful music that makes, a music born of pain, furious hope, of recklessness, the desire for transformation. The woman of 'Night Waitress' desires a song to fill her wildly, powerfully, that kind of romance that's ultimately illusory. In 'Midnight Reports' music's anarchic, and really what I'm hearing most there is the soundtrack to the riots of '67 and '68, a blown-up shattered-glass black sound—the music I grew up with—powered nevertheless by desperate style, by grace."

RICHARD JACKSON teaches at the University of Tennessee, Chattanooga, where he edits *The Poetry Miscellany* and the *Poetry Miscellany* Eastern European Chapbook series. A winner of many teaching awards, two Pushcart prizes, an NEA fellowship, a Fulbright fellowship, and numerous other awards, he is the author of three books of poems, most recently *Alive All Day*. His poems have appeared in several anthologies here and abroad. In addition, he has written two critical books and edited *Four Slovene Poets*.

"'Eight Ball' began, literally, as it does on paper, for I was thinking at the time that I was sort of living inside the poem. It reminded me of years ago in a similar bar in New York when I was pretending to study to be an engineer, and so the references to Lorca, I suppose, and the fact that I had begun reading him again. There was a while in college when I was a pretty fair pool player, but I learned that night several years ago and since that those days are long gone. But there's something about the satisfaction of pulling off an occasional exceptional shot that has poetry in it—the parts come together, the ball falls cleanly at the end, and all of a sudden the disparate pieces that seemed scattered all over the table like the bits and pieces in my notebook suddenly come together. Just as in the songs, the ballads especially, the sadder the better, that I loved in college and high school. So of course, there's the music—country and western, pop—I was discovering the roots of rock and roll and loving it, and that too was coming together like a nice combination shot to the side pocket. I had this feeling all the time that I was dancing, not walking around the table."

MARK JARMAN, who grew up in Redondo Beach, California, is the author of five books of poetry: *North Sea, The Rote Walker, Far and Away, The Black Riviera,* and *Iris,* a book-length poem. He has received grants from the Guggenheim Foundation and the NEA. He lives in Nashville with his wife and daughters and teaches at Vanderbilt University.

"'The Supremes' is about discovering and listening to Motown music, that hybrid of rhythm and blues and soul created by Barry Gordy and the songwriters Holland, Dozier, and Holland. It is also about the beach culture of Southern California in the mid-sixties and my realization that the music of the Supremes, for example, with its simple, effective beat and sweet, heartbroken melodies, and not the surf music of the local bands, was what I felt in the life I was living. I have long since learned it was not an unusual experience for a white kid to discover black music made by black singers and musicians and to want either to be part of it or at least to make it part of his life. Of course, the lives of Diana Ross, Mary Wilson, and Florence Ballard were culturally as well as geographically distant from mine. (I could hardly picture Detroit.) But their music arrived where I lived by the airwaves of radio and TV and was complemented by the waves coming to shore in Santa Monica Bay. Thinking back on those waves and that place, I think of that music; hearing that music, I think of that place and those waves."

DENIS JOHNSON's books include *Angels, Fiskadoro, The Stars at Noon, The Veil,* and *The Incognito Lounge.*

DAVID KELLER grew up in Ames, Iowa. His poems like to claim that he was educated in the theaters and orchestra pits of the Boston area, although he studied at Harvard and at the University of Wisconsin. His most recent book, *Land That Wasn't Ours*, will be followed by *In the New World*.

"Bill Matthews once theorized that, prior to rock and roll, adolescents weren't expected/thought to have feelings, since they were mostly inarticulate about them. The music gave them/us a way to express feelings."

YUSEF KOMUNYAKAA's most recent collection of poetry, *Neon Vernacular*, won the 1994 Kingsley Tufts Poetry Award. He has been the Holloway Lecturer at the University of California, Berkeley, and presently teaches creative writing at Indiana University.

"Irony underlies the rock and roll references in these two Vietnam-related poems. The realities of American history pulsate underneath them, a reminder that racism is still with us—from Benny Goodman as the King of Swing to Elvis as the King of Rock and Roll."

SYDNEY LEA, author of five poetry collections, most recently *The Blainville Testament* and *Prayer for the Little City*, has also published a novel, *A Place in Mind*, and is at work on a collection of naturalist essays. The recipient of fellowships from the Guggenheim, Rockefeller, and Fulbright foundations, he was founder and, for thirteen years, editor of the *New England Review*. He is a member of the MFA faculty at Vermont College.

"'The One White Face in the Place': My late adolescence and early adulthood were deeply devoted not so much to rock and roll as to its parents, pure blues and so-called rhythm and blues. I *would* indeed 'travel across three states' to hear my favorites. Fate consigned me—though I don't in the least complain—to pure white upper New England, and in this poem, as so often, I've had occasion to wonder whether there were any connections between my early, largely African-American 'influences' (which have in all candor proved far more profound than conventionally literary ones) and the emphatically Yankee surroundings I've known for twenty-five years. 'The One White Face in the Place' explores this matter both formally and thematically.

"'Tempted by the Classical on Returning from the Store at Twenty below Zero': At its finest, rock and roll, like blues, may accept received forms (the twelve-bar measure, the 1-5-4-1 chord progression), but insists on bending them—even to the point of subversion. Pseudo–rock and roll honors form alone (like certain bloodless contemporary poetry): no 'funk' remains. The brawl of life can tempt us to do the same in our personal existences, to crave the order of an empty 'classicism.' To that extent, Debbie Boone's nauseatingly saccharine and 'easy' 'You Light Up My Life' is a model of such an essentially resigned posture toward the world—a posture that freezes both mind and body. What the speaker of my poem really could use is a fit of Huey 'Piano' Smith's rockin' pneumonia and boogie-woogie flu."

LARRY LEVIS's books include *Winter Stars, The Afterlife, The Dollmaker's Ghost,* and *Wrecking Crew.*

RACHEL LODEN's poems are forthcoming in *New American Writing,* the *Kansas Quarterly,* and the *Green Mountains Review* and have appeared in the *New York Quarterly, Poet & Critic,* and *The Quarterly,* among others. She lives in Palo Alto, California.
"'I thought all your walled cities / would fall / to rock & roll. . . .' Against the insults and uncertainties peculiar to loving is posed this music, which is only the most passionate thing I know. The songs are like amulets in the poem—rattling their power to heal and to overcome—but the singer here is forced to admit the limitations of that power, the necessity and even the pleasure of her uncertainty."

ROBERT LONG, born in 1954 in New York City, is the author of *What Happens* and the forthcoming *Terminal Cafe,* among other collections. His work has appeared in the *New Yorker, Poetry,* and other journals, and he has taught at various institutions, including Long Island University and LaSalle University.
"John Ashbery once remarked somewhere that he thought of titles as key signatures: they tilted the poem in a certain direction. That's usually how titles work for me, and I'll often have a title lying around long before I find a poem to hook it to. I'm a longtime fan of Elvis Costello, and I knew I had to borrow the title of his great song for a poem; how the title relates to the poem exactly, I'm not sure, but I know that it fits.

For me, as for a lot of poets of my generation, rock and roll opened aesthetic doors; certainly, when I was a kid starting out, Jim Morrison's use of language ("gazing on a city under television skies") was more responsible for exciting me into poetry than was any poetry I happened to be reading. I'd still rather drive my car a little too fast on a summer day over country roads with the windows down with Elvin C. or Miles Davis or George Clinton—the three who are in the glove compartment today—blaring from the speakers than read, oh, let's just say 'a lot' of what passes for poetry in these increasingly airless days for the art."

B. D. LOVE currently teaches composition at California State University in Los Angeles as well as writes music and plays for Bukowski's Children, a postdeconstructionist rock and roll band.

"I chose to write 'Bryan Ferry' in the sonnet form because, after all, the sonnet is a 'little song,' and as such it stands as enduring proof that *less* very often conveys *more*, that apparent simplicity can signify strength, not weakness. Many people don't understand that pop songwriting is a very formal craft, often as structurally demanding as composing a verse sonnet. Bryan Ferry certainly understands this. His later work with his band, Roxy Music, and on his own reveals a highly polished craftsmanship that we often don't associate with rock and roll. I wrote this small poem to honor Ferry's songwriting as well as his vocal artistry."

CHARLES LYNCH, born in Baltimore, attended both Kenyon College and the City College of New York and completed his doctoral dissertation, on the poetry of Robert Hayden and Gwendolyn Brooks, at New York University. His poems have appeared in *The Poetry of Black America: Anthology of the 20th Century, Leaving the Bough: Fifty American Poets of the the Eighties,* and *Long Journey Home: A Poetry Anthology* and in many periodicals, such as *Chelsea,* the *Yardbird Reader, Hanging Loose, Obsidian,* the *Greenfield Review,* and *Black American Literature Forum.* He is a freelance writer and editor.

"'Ancestral Echoes / Rap Music' celebrates rappers' ability to integrate a variety of sounds, gestures, and roles featured in the African and African-American secular and religious heritage: bebopper, griot, exhortatory preacher and enthralled congregation, dozens player, wandering blues minstrel, Nigerian talking drum, deep-voiced soul singer, the 'bad man' hero. Percussive vocalisms at the microphone can imitate a jug band, and the D.J.'s turntables conjure sounds that remind me of soft-shoe dancing on a sandy floor or a chakere (beaded gourd) being shaken and slapped."

WALTER MCDONALD, Paul Whitfield Horn Professor of English and Poet-in-Residence at Texas Tech University, has published thirteen collections of poems, including *After the Noise of Saigon, The Flying Dutchman,* and *Night Landings.* His poems have appeared in the *Atlantic, The Nation,* the *New York Review of Books,* the *Paris Review,* and *Poetry.* Two other books received the National Cowboy Hall of Fame's Western Heritage Award—*The Digs in Escondido Canyon* in 1992 and *Rafting the Brazos* in 1990.

"Growing up in West Texas, a prairie town more famous for cotton and Buddy Holly than opera, I cut my teeth on country-and-western jukebox ballads and local steel-guitar bands. Hard-thumping drums and bitter-sweet guitars must have been cradle music in Lubbock; the songs sad fellows whined riding away into the sunset gave us a tough code of coping. They sang as if no one was around to hear them under a thousand miles of stars; but their lessons of lonesome love were best practiced over and over in somebody's arms after the dust of sandstorms, in spite of wars and rumors of wars and ordinary losses."

MICHAEL MCFEE'S books include *Vanishing Acts, Sad Girl Sitting on a Running Board,* and *To See,* the latter a collaboration with photographer Elizabeth Matheson. He has been a visiting poet at Cornell, the University of North Carolina at Lawrence, and Chapel Hill. He lives in Durham, North Carolina.

"'First Radio' is about the first radio I owned, a cheap transistor that could nevertheless pull in the glamorous Big World Out There, which seemed so remote when growing up in the North Carolina mountains in the early 1960s. Chief among that World's attractions were baseball's annual Series and especially rock and roll music, which I'd listen to at night on WOWO, Fort Wayne, Indiana, when I was supposed to be saying my prayers in bed like any good Southern Baptist boy."

KATHARYN HOWD MACHAN has published several collections of her poetry: *When She Was the Good-Time Girl,* winner of the 1986 Signpost Press competition; *From Redwing; Redwing Women,* winner of the 1988 CrazyQuilt Press competition; and *The Kitchen of Your Dreams,* which received the Goodman Award. She teaches in the Writing Program of Ithaca College.

PAUL MCRAY has published a chapbook, *As Though Traveling Backwards Were Natural,* and his poems have appeared widely in journals, including the *Antioch Review, Poetry,* and *Poetry Northwest.* He lives in Strafford, Vermont, with his wife and their daughter, Annie.

"The girl in 'Performance,' like so many of her generation, like Janis Joplin herself, flew right off the planet in search of an escape from a world shot through with decay. The dramatic context of the poem is meant to echo the widespread process of immolation that was often performed on the altar of Rock and Roll. The men in the bar are of course celebrating their own version of the same service—coming up next on the jukebox: 'In the Mood.'"

PAUL MARIANI'S most recent books are *Salvage Operations: New and Selected Poems* and *Dream Song: The Life of John Berryman.* At present he is working on a critical biography of Robert Lowell, a book of essays, and another book of poems.

"For me 'Betty' still elicits a complex of emotions. The time was the late summer of 1957. I was seventeen, and had just completed a year at the Marianist Preparatory in Beacon, New York. I remember being assigned to a work crew to pull out tree stumps at the Preparatory one day the previous fall. By religious rule we should have worked in silence. But it was a warm afternoon, the end of summer falling with that mid-October day, perhaps eight of us, young men aged fourteen to eighteen, a forbidden radio softly playing rock and roll, the young Presley's 'Love Me Tender' the only song I can distinctly recall now. And though one of the young men pursed his lips and tried to block out the music, no one reported us that day.

"For two hours I dreamt the scents of summer: fresh-mown grass, cut hay, wild berries, the faint perfume of a girl in a summery dress off in a field somewhere, while I pickaxed and roped the stump I'd been assigned until it yielded. There was a plangency about the invisible words, the simple melodies, those sweet nothings, which it seems impossible to convey to a younger generation brought up on the urgencies, despairs, and social sophistications of rap and heavy metal. The lyrics of rock and roll have about them something unintentionally comic, naive, gossamer, triste, unrepeatable.

"In 'Betty' I had my first taste of dating again, just weeks after I'd decided—after a hell of hesitations—that I wasn't going to go back to the seminary. Betty was a local girl, quiet, Baptist, incredibly sweet, as innocent as myself. Nothing much happened in the back seat of Grippie's Ford, except what a young man's ardent desire (coupled with an all-pervasive guilt) and a Catholic imagination could bring to such a wished-for consummation (by which I mean the intimation of a kiss, an awkward embrace). When one's own sons are already older than the young man in the poem, and one's best friend has already succumbed to the insistent vicissitudes of death, one looks back on such gardenia-scented moments as that in 'Betty' with more than a touch of nostalgia and wonder, mixed now with the briny taste of knowledge.

"One sees on television the ads for cassettes or CDs collecting the best of these old rock and roll songs, sees the reenacted scenes of flared skirts and bobby socks, boys sporting crew cuts and D.A.s, the store-bought picture of some barn or ship on the finished basement wall of a friend's house, the Coke bottles and chips, and one smiles. Smiles, before the intervening thirty years and more come crashing down, the way one remembers coal rumbling down the chute towards the waiting bin."

WILLIAMS MATTHEWS's many books include *Foreseeable Futures* and *A Happy Childhood.*

LISEL MUELLER is the author of five books of poetry, as well as four books of poetry and prose in translation. In 1990 she published *Learning to Play by Ear,* a volume of essays and early poems.

"'The Deaf Dancing to Rock' has two sources. One is my preoccupation with Helen Keller, who 'listened' to music by putting her hands against the speaker of a radio. The other is a statement by Jerry Garcia of the Grateful Dead, who said the deaf enjoyed rock music so much because it was amplified and they can feel the vibrations in the floor."

KAY MURPHY teaches at the University of New Orleans. Her poetry has appeared in the *Spoon River Quarterly* and the *New York Quarterly,* her fiction in *Fiction International* and *Ascent.* Her first book of poetry was *The Autopsy.* She is looking for a publisher for her second, *Belief Is Getting More Difficult,* and finishing a collection of short stories, *Living on the Parade Route.*

"Andrei Codrescu once said, 'It ain't rock 'n' roll but it ain't death either,' and in the heat of my adolescence, I felt just that: Give me rock and roll or give me death, because nothing in the middle mattered. In 'Eighties Meditation' I try to capture the shift in attitude between the rock and roll of Hendrix's 'Purple Haze,' which could not be distinguished from a hit of acid or a hit of god, and the eighties' music, which seems to have no vision beyond a consciousness of materialism and violence. I don't believe that the same people who listen to early rock are also the ones who say, 'FUCK THE WORLD.'

"In *The Poetry of Rock* David Pichaske says, 'The moment of rock as a socio-political force and as poetry is ended'; thus 'The Girl with the Bad Rep' is not only an elegy for the type of girl depicted in the poem, personified as a 'sister,' but an elegy for rock and roll 'like any other romance, over.' This poem picks up the same theme as 'Eighties Meditation' in its expression of the urgency in 'Dance / or drop dead.' It's a recent poem, which indicates I still hold these beliefs."

ROCHELLE NAMEROFF is a 1992 recipient of an NEA Fellowship in Creative Writing for creative nonfiction as well as of a 1991 Iowa Arts Council Fellowship in Poetry. Her poetry has appeared in many journals, including the *Antioch Review,* the *Denver Quarterly,* and *Poetry Northwest.* She is Assistant Professor of English at the University of Scranton.

"Both poems are part of a sequence called 'Medley'; other poems in 'Medley' range from Judy Garland and Fred Astaire to the Beatles, the Everly Brothers to piano lessons, camp songs, and my parents' music.

"Music often seems the ground of my life, not just soundtrack and nostalgia, but texture and warmth and spirit. Music is the opening and gathering place of memory, where re-call and re-collection of the many layers of the past takes place, the mouth the seductive entry to the gods of the body and the soul. I write about music because it has moved me more than all the statuary in the world. 'Oh Orpheus sings! Oh tall tree in the ear!'"

JOYCE CAROL OATES's most recent collection of poetry is *The Time Traveler: Poems, 1983–1989*. She lives and teaches in Princeton, New Jersey.
    "'Waiting on Elvis, 1956' is really about the loss of youth and innocence—the old days of rock and roll, gone forever."

FRANK O'HARA (1926–1966) published only a few, small-press collections of his poetry before his untimely death. His *Collected Poems, Selected Poems, Poems Retrieved*, and *Early Writing*, all edited by Donald Allen, were published posthumously.

ROBERT PHILLIPS is the author of five books of poetry, including *Personal Accounts: New and Selected Poems, 1966–86*, for which he received an Award in Literature from the American Academy and Institute of Arts and Letters, and a chapbook of poems, *Face to Face*. Currently, he is Director of the Creative Writing Program and Professor of English at the University of Houston.
    "'The Death of Janis Joplin' is one of the very few poems I ever wrote on commission. An editor asked me to contribute to an anthology of poems based upon events of the 1960s, and I had none. For all the traumas of that decade—the Americanization of the Vietnam War, the assassinations of both Kennedys as well as Dr. King—I somehow settled upon the life and death of Joplin instead. Her death by self-administered overdose seemed to epitomize the decade's waste. And I admired her 'style.' She was a superstar capable of self-deprecation, as when she introduced 'Oh Lord, Won't You Buy Me a Mercedes Benz' with the words, 'Now here's a song of great cosmic import. . . .'
    "Her album *Pearl* had a great effect on me. I'm not convinced Joplin is directly related to rock and roll the way Lennon and McCartney, Bob Dylan, or the Doors are. The power and sadness of her singing seem more related to the Negro blues tradition of Bessie Smith and Billie Holiday. Perhaps she was the personification of Norman Mailer's invention, 'The White Negro.' Whatever she was, we miss her."

JIM POWELL's first collection of poems was *It Was Fever That Made the*

World. His translation of the complete extant poems and fragments of Sappho was published in 1993. He lives in Berkeley.

"One catalyst for 'It Was Fever That Made the World' was the Jerry Garcia Band jamming on Roy Hamilton's R&B hit 'Don't Let Go' at the Stone in San Francisco on August 24, 1984, but the poem as a whole invokes rock less for its own sake than as an accompaniment or instigation to dance and to agapic communal revelry, particularly as it arises in a small club between an attentive dancing audience and musicians playing improvisational rock. Here, when the energy is right, it is through the dancers' bodies that 'the music plays the band.' King Pentheus is always sending around his uniformed perverts to shut down Dionysus' nightclubs because, to him, this feverish physical and psychic interplay looks like a disease—and an especially threatening one because it presents him with the infuriating spectacle of his subjects violating his Law's primal insistence on their absolutely disjunct and isolated 'individuality,' divided and conquered by the cash nexus. This is the basis in reality of the radicalism of rock; it has nothing to do with the 'music business,' which is just another gang of Pentheus' henchmen (see Dylan's comments in the notes to *Biograph*)."

THOMAS REITER's most recent collection of poetry is *Completing the New Lake*. He is Wayne D. McMurray Professor of Humanities at Monmouth College in New Jersey.

"The reference in 'Class Bully' to 'Rock around the Clock' has to do with the relationship between the class bully and those grade-school classmates who both fear and admire him. They hope that in his new role as sexton (given to him by the Mother Superior in an attempt to break his rebellious spirit) he will ring out that Bill Haley song, but instead he rings the steeple bells in a perfectly appropriate way. Thus he has been diminished, lost to authority."

TAD RICHARDS currently lives in Saugerties, New York, where he is President of the Board of Trustees of Opus 40, Inc., a regional arts organization. His poetry has appeared in the *Laurel Review* and the *Carolina Quarterly*. His book *The New Country Encyclopedia* was published in 1993, and his songs have appeared on recent albums by Orleans, John Hall, and Fred Koller.

"The relationship of 'Challenge to the Reader' to rock and roll is the relationship of my life to rock and roll, especially early rock and roll: its words, its rhythms are at all times part of who I am, how I relate to my world and my inner landscape. As a scared and isolated teenager in the fifties, living in what I knew was not the real world, the words and the emotional text of Ray Charles and Little Richard, the Cleftones and the Moonglows, were messages to me from a world I knew existed somewhere. If I could pay close attention, I might find the key to that world.

"So in 'Challenge to the Reader,' trying to understand an emotional mystery which I fraudulently claim to have completely unraveled, I turned to the wonderful mystery-solving bravado of Lieber and Stoller and the Coasters—but undercut the emotional sureness of it by undercutting its rhythmic certainty and recasting it in my own halting syllabics."

JACK RIDL has published two collections, *The Same Ghost* and *Between,* and his poems have appeared in *Poetry East,* the *Denver Quarterly, Yarrow,* and *Poetry,* among other journals. He lives at Ottawa Beach along Lake Michigan.

"My mother stormed the stage at a Frank Sinatra concert when she was a teenager. She made sure we saw the Beatles. And in her late sixties she became a Springsteen fan. She has gone to his concerts, sitting in the tenth row, has everything by him and about him and wears a black Springsteen T-shirt."

DAVID RIVARD was born in Fall River, Massachusetts, in 1953. His poems have appeared in *Poetry, Ploughshares,* the *North American Review, Agni,* and other magazines. *Torque,* his first book of poems, won the 1987 Agnes Lynch Starrett Poetry Prize and was published in the Pitt Poetry Series in 1988. Among his awards are fellowships in poetry from the National Endowment for the Arts (1986 and 1991) and from the Fine Arts Work Center in Provincetown. He teaches at Tufts University and in the M.F.A. in Writing Program at Vermont College.

"As Bob Dylan once said, 'with a certain kind of blues music, you can sit down and play it . . . you may have to lean forward a little.' That's always seemed like a fine thing to me, a good thing to have to do."

NANCY SCHOENBERGER has published a collection of her poems, *Girl on a White Porch*.

JAMES SEAY's most recent collection of poetry is *The Light as They Found It*. He teaches at the University of North Carolina at Chapel Hill.

"As much as I hate to admit it, my poem 'Johnny B. Goode' wasn't actually prompted by the high-speed, low-drag frenzy of the music itself. Well, maybe you could trace it *back* to that, when the octane of 'Maybelline' or 'Johnny B. Goode' hit my pistons for the first time, but that's stretching it. What got me started on the poem was enervatingly cerebral, I'm afraid. I started thinking on how there's no clear and definite resolution or, dare I say, *dénouement* in the narrative structure of some of Chuck Berry's songs. We know that Johnny is more than nominally good and that he will honor his mother's dream—become the leader of a big ol' band and see his name in lights—but, strictly speaking, the song leaves that outcome tentative. I know and you know that that is what will surely happen, but the song doesn't actually come out and say that things work out that way for Johnny. Or that he achieves fame and then starts longing for the lost Eden of his childhood home way back up in the woods among the evergreens. More interesting, though, is how in 'Maybelline,' after the rain gets up under the hero's hood and does his motor good and he pulls his V-8 Ford up over the hill and alongside the Coupe de Ville in which Maybelline is two-timing him with another man, nothing really happens. The hero just asks Maybelline—through his open window, one assumes—why can't she be true. And at the same time, maybe by way of reminding himself it's not his fault, observes for her that she has done started back doing the things she used to do. That's it; no straight razors, no Uzis, no crash-and-burn suicide-murder on the open road. Don't misunderstand; I am stunned with the narrative genius, not to mention poignancy, of all this. It is worthy of Chekhov. But it isn't your traditionally cathartic narrative fare. That is, if you think about it at the wrong time, it could interfere with your dancing. On second thought, just forget I ever wrote any of this. It's not like I don't understand what Mr. Charles Berry said in 'School Days.' *Hail, hail, rock and roll. Deliver me from the days of old. Long live rock and roll. . . . The feeling is there, body and soul.*

"In my poem 'Audubon Drive, Memphis' I'm not thinking so much about the music of rock and roll as about the way rock stars get hurled into systems of gratification they rarely know how to negotiate with, short of excess. But more than that I'm thinking about how we get so vicariously intimate with them and other public figures whose candlepower we choose as part of the illumination of our own hopes. It's an old story, of course, only now it's fiberoptic and laser-beamed, and tomorrow it may be virtual-reality computer-driven. At any rate, we know their addresses, diets, and designers of choice. In some instances we remember where we were when they died. We're that close. In the case of Elvis, I wasn't, despite what the poem implies, parked outside a gas station / just over the bridge from Pawley's Island / with the radio on. That's just the way I scripted it, knowing what I know of Elvis's life. The cars and all, I mean. Actually I was on Pawley's Island, in a convenience store, buying some orange juice for breakfast, and I saw the newspaper headline THE KING IS DEAD. When JFK and Martin Luther King were killed, I was where I say I was in the poem. I wept both times, but that doesn't keep them out of the overlap with Elvis, for whom I was sorry but not moved to tears. So there they are together, at least in the economy I've imagined, still waiting for the pool to fill. And we know more or less everything that is happening to them."

ALEDA SHIRLEY has published *Chinese Architecture* and a chapbook, *Silver Ending,* winner of the 1991 Hanks Chapbook Award.

DAN SICOLI, cofounder and coeditor of *Slipstream* magazine and press, spent seven years banging out guitar chords in a local rock and roll band in every dive and on every stage in town during the 1980s. He presently works in community development.
"My poem is my reaction to the 'death' of rock and roll. The jolt of life it received during the mid-to-late 1970s with the punk movement was just a flash in the pan."

JACK SKELLEY is poet, journalist, and musician. As the latter, he recorded two albums on SST Records with the instrumental rock band Lawndale.
"Pop culture, including rock and roll, potato chips, and the transfor-

mative powers of porno queens on the evolution of sexual conscious-
ness, is, or should be, *the* theme of poetry."

FLOYD SKLOOT's first collection of poems, *Music Appreciation*, was pub-
lished in 1993. He is also author of a novel, *Pilgrim's Harbor*. His work
has appeared in *Harper's, Poetry, Shenandoah, Prairie Schooner*, the
American Scholar, and the *Virginia Quarterly Review*.

"When I was growing up in Brooklyn, New York, in the fifties, I didn't
just listen to rock and roll. Rock and roll was part of my life in the
same way the Dodgers, early television, and being a Polio Pioneer in
1954 were part of my life. I absorbed them. We gave and took from
each other. They helped me define the world in which I found myself."

BRUCE SMITH, author of two books of poems, *The Common Wages* and
Silver and Information, has had his work published in *Paris Review,
Grand Street*, the *Partisan Review, TLS*, and the *Agni Review*. He once
danced with the Coasters.

"The title 'How Garnett Mims and the Enchanters Came into Your
Life' is a reference to the style of evangelical 'testifying'—the sworn
evidence of how the spirit with its tongue of fire licks and changes
us—the kind of thing you might hear over the radio at 3 A.M. driving
across Texas. 'Cry, Cry Baby' and 'For Your Precious Love' were Garnett
Mims's two most popular recordings. These heartbreaking, devotional
songs of high sentiment and extravagant emotional richness are set
against the boredom and routine of school with its textbooks and
fractions. The immediately identifiable revivalist song—stylized and
smuggled—was taboo, sexual cargo, racial otherness, and defiance of
all father authority as transporting as prayer. The rest is just Pop-bob-
a-lama, pop-a-lam-bam-boo."

GARY SOTO's many books include *Black Hair, The Elements of San
Joaquin, The Tale of Sunlight*, and *Where Sparrows Work Hard*.

RICHARD SPEAKES lives and works in Santa Rosa, California.

"When I was a boy, rock and roll was a sort of religion to me, perhaps
a sad fact. But strange and miraculous energies attended it, and they
were generous, satisfied to use me, and central to my life is this: rather
than playing that music, I talked about it whenever I had the chance.

Unaccountable joy that doesn't shy from evil—nearly all early Jerry Lee Lewis, for instance—is naturally enough an ally, even a muse. That rock and roll is a white-trash muse is helpful for someone writing poems, an activity that can so easily become precious."

DAVID ST. JOHN is the author of four collections of poetry, *Hush, The Shore, No Heaven,* and *Terraces of Rain,* as well as three limited-edition books, *The Olive Grove, The Orange Piano,* and *The Unsayable, The Unknowable, and You.* He is Poetry Editor of the *Antioch Review* and Professor of English at the University of Southern California.

"'California' is a poem that began while I was gambling in a casino in Lake Tahoe. It was summer in the mid-1970s. Behind me, while I was playing blackjack, the unmistakable driving beat of Bo Diddley and his band began. Without knowing it, I'd been playing cards with my back to the small theater in the casino. As I turned around, the stage curtain opened to reveal Bo and the gang, thumping away on the pulse of 'Who Do You Love.' It's a song that has always identified for me the urgency of sexual desire, its confusion and pain. A few weeks later, when I began to write the poem about the illicit affair between the couple in 'California,' I knew from the start what its epigraph had to be.

"As a teenager I used to play in rock and roll bands. I played (in various bands) electric bass (Fender six-string, through an old tube-model, blond Bassman amp), the organ (Farfisa), and/or guitar (Gibson Hummingbird acoustic, Guild and Rickenbacker electrics). To be perfectly candid about it, the only instrument I was really any good on was the bass. I had begun at thirteen as a folkie, then came the Byrds, the Who, the Stones, and I started rocking. But from the beginning, I'd been obsessed by the Delta Blues. Blind Lemon Jefferson and Robert Johnson were the two singers I loved most. I spent most of one especially difficult year of my life listening to Robert Johnson and drinking pots of espresso until I was wired out of my skull. Robert Johnson's was the only music desperate enough to make any sense to me. I've been listening to Robert Johnson for more than twenty-five years now. He is the Blake of the blues."

KEVIN STEIN's first collection, *A Circus of Want,* won the Devins Award. He has authored a critical study as well, *James Wright: The Poetry of a Grown Man.* He teaches at Bradley University.

"One face burnished with possibility, the other contorted with despair, the two-headed god Promise and Loss visited my parents' house, transmogrified into the voice of rock and roll. It spoke to me from their Magnavox, in high-fidelity. Spotlighted beneath the kliegs, a lead singer lilted 'All things are possible,' while in the shadows, back-ups swayed as they offered the haunting refrain and rejoinder, 'No they ain't' ('ain't' being part rebellion, part posture, part untutored American genius).

"It's fair to say rock and roll is popular culture's epic of innocence and experience. Its compulsive theme: awakenings of the sexual, social, political, and emotional variety. If my parents were raised on Basie, Ellington, and the splendid Glenn Miller and then smashed headlong into World War II, we who crooned fifties ditties had Vietnam, Kent State, and the Civil Rights movement. Much of our music echoed that crush and the anger which ensued, and still insistently urged upon us an alternative rebirth. Naively perhaps, given the state of things.

"Maybe it's only the sad admission of a lost classical education, maybe just a passing fancy, but many poems carry with them, if only unconsciously, my weak impersonation of guitar riff, drum solo, background vocals, and someone singing words as close to song as he can reach."

ALISON STONE's work has appeared in *Poetry*, the *Paris Review*, *Ploughshares*, the *New Statesman*, and a variety of other journals and anthologies. She received her Master's in Writing from NYU. She is also a painter.

"*Rocket to Russia* is the title of a Ramones album, and the whole poem is about 'the punk rock scene.' 'Spofford Hall' suggests that drugs and rock are both attempts to achieve freedom, though music works better in the long run."

SUSAN SWARTWOUT's poetry has appeared in the *Mississippi Review*, *Sou'wester*, the *Nebraska Review*, *Cape Rock*, and other journals. Assistant Editor of the *Spoon River Quarterly*, she teaches at Illinois State University.

"'I Wannabe Your Queen' exists because of a friend's challenge for me to write a Bad Elvis Poem. To compose, I had to come to grips with some definition of Bad Elvis, and I decided that 'bad peom' had to include elements of historical poems we were all force-read in high school and which, a few years later, became *verboten* in our writing—heroic couplets, heightened language, Capitalized Concepts, etc. Also included in the Elvis poem is the dread iambic tetrameter, and if you give it a college try, you can sing the poem to the tune of 'Be My Little Teddy Bear.' The poem attempts to embody Queen for a Day or lotto mentality—the fantasy that somewhere, perhaps at the carnival or on the beach or racetrack, some rubberlipped god would toss back an ebony forelock, pull you to his pelvis, and whisper in your ear, 'Viva Las Vegas!'"

DAVID TRINIDAD's most recent book is *Hand over Heart: Poems, 1981–1988*. His poetry has appeared in numerous magazines and anthologies, including *Harper's*, the *Paris Review, New American Writing*, and *Best American Poetry 1991*. He lives in New York City.

"In '"Monday, Monday"' I wanted to explore, among other things, the feeling that comes over me when I hear certain songs I listened to as a teenager. Anne Sexton described it perfectly in her poem 'Music Swims Back to Me': 'Music pours over the sense / and in a funny way / music sees more than I. / I mean it remembers better. . . .' Such songs as the Mamas and the Papas' 'Monday, Monday,' Sonny and Cher's 'I Got You Babe,' and Jan and Dean's 'The Little Old Lady (from Pasadena)' can instantly pull me, against my will, back to the mid-sixties; the music remembers, more than I do, all the confusion and pain of adolescence.

"I've always thought of '*Meet the Supremes*' as a kind of 'list narrative,' an attempt to celebrate, as well as demystify, my identification and obsession with rock and roll girls—their big hair and go-go boots, their plaintive tales of heartbreak and betrayal, and (most important) their incessant 'Da Doo Ron Ron's' and 'Doo-lang Doo-lang's.' My angst, of course, is masked by nothing more than a layer of white lipstick. The roll call about a third of the way through is meant to interrupt the poem like a song, an enchanting new hit on my transistor radio."

JUDITH VOLLMER's first book of poems, *Level Green*, won the 1990 Brittingham Prize. Her poems, interviews, and reviews have appeared in many magazines. She lives in Pittsburgh and teaches creative writing at the University of Pittsburgh at Greensburg.

"These poems were inspired by alley grit, kitchen grease, and second-hand amplifiers—that is, by women making rock music over the last twenty-five years. Because rock is constantly dying and renewing itself, it makes room for sounds and voices coming to first articulation. From our cities and our desires we build poetries not as fixed icons but as fires buring in the *real*."

RONALD WALLACE, born in Cedar Rapids, Iowa, in 1945, grew up in St. Louis, Missouri. His eight books include *The Makings of Happiness, People and Dog in the Sun,* and *God Be with the Clown: Humor in American Poetry.* Director of Creative Writing at the University of Wisconsin–Madison and Series Editor for the University of Wisconsin Press's Brittingham Prize in Poetry, he divides his time between Madison and a forty-acre farm in Bear Valley, Wisconsin.

"Whenever my fifteen-year-old daughter is with me in the car, we fight over the radio. Surreptitiously, she'll switch it to the local rap and hard rock station; surreptitiously, I'll switch it back to my oldies. She complains that all my songs sound the same, that she can sing any of them even if she has never heard them before. She thinks all those old songs are stupid. And, in fact, they are: simple-minded, sentimental, unsophisticated, innocent, and I know them all by heart and they bring tears to my eyes, King of Nostalgia that I am.

"Music is such a powerful mnemonic force. Like poetry, it saves the past, confers an immortality on experience, defies the authority of time and forgetfulness. The Dell-Vikings, the Diamonds, Buddy Holly, the Big Bopper, Jimmy Rogers didn't just sing songs, they orchestrated my life at a time when I was discovering love and sex and death and the vagaries of the great world. My sixth-grade girlfriend, the pastor's son, my father's illness are inextricably interfused with the music. It brings it all back.

"Sometimes I wonder if my daughter's music will do that for her. If thirty years from now she'll hear something by Two Live Crew or Ice T and be transported back to all the sad sweetness of these moments in her life. Maybe. But somehow I kind of doubt it. *Diiii-yi-yi-yi-yi. Dip-da-dip-dip. Sha-na-na-na-sha-na-na-na.*"

DOYLE WESLEY WALLS teaches at Pacific University. His writings appear in such publications as *Poet & Critic,* the *New York Quarterly, Modern Drama,* and *American Literature.* He wants to be a paperback writer.

"I first heard 'Hey Jude' and 'Revolution' while sitting in the back of my parents' Delta 88 on vacation in New Orleans. When I bought the single, I noticed that the familiar yellow and orange swirl on my Beatles singles from Capitol Records had disappeared. 'Hey Jude' had, instead, a green apple, and 'Revolution' had the apple sliced down the middle.

"Many years later I relished watching, in Patrick Montgomery's fine documentary *The Compleat Beatles,* John Lennon at a press conference, announcing into the microphones of some major corporations, and with some contempt, the formation of the Beatles' new company, Apple Corp., 'a company,' in the words of the narrator of the documentary, 'to be run by themselves and for themselves.' The Beatles had broken away from their parent company, Capitol, and created their own. In those days, radio usually refused to play a song over three minutes long. 'Hey Jude,' at seven minutes and eleven seconds, was the Beatles' first release from Apple Records and their largest-selling single of all.

"What I knew then was that those songs had great sounds and words that embodied energy, intimacy, sex, world consciousness, change.

"What I came to know later was this: The Beatles' desire for creative control, as expressed in the facts surrounding the release of 'Hey Jude/ Revolution,' paralleled my own awakening in my adolescence to the myriad moves anyone could make once he had grown up and away from parental control (however wise, however tolerant), once he was the artist of his own life."

MICHAEL WATERS teaches at Salisbury State University on the Eastern Shore of Maryland. His recent books include *Bountiful, The Burden Lifters,* and *Anniversary of the Air.* In 1986, as lead singer of Michael and the G-Spots, he released his own composition, "(Say Goodbye to Your) Summer Boyfriend."

"'*American Bandstand*' was written during 1981–82 while I was living in Athens, Greece, and both missing and gaining some perspective on American pop culture. During the fifties and early sixties, Dick Clark's *American Bandstand* was less important for the platters spun than for the dances made popular. To anyone approaching or mired in adolescence, those dances seemed the key to social success. 'The Burden

Lifters' means to affirm the power of music—in this case, gospel—to heal. Rock and roll remains rooted in the church."

WARREN WOESSNER, Senior Editor of *Abraxas* magazine, has worked as a soul/R&B DJ at WORT-FM, Madison, Wisconsin. His most recent collection of poetry is *Storm Lines.*

DAVID WOJAHN, author of three collections of poems, *Icehouse Lights, Glassworks,* and *Mystery Train,* has received the William Carlos Williams Book Award, the Yale Series of Younger Poets Prize, and the George Kent Memorial Prize from *Poetry,* as well as fellowships from the NEA, the Fine Arts Work Center in Provincetown, and the Amy Lowell Travelling Poetry Scholarship Fund. He teaches creative writing at Indiana University and in the MFA in Writing Program of Vermont College.

"Rock and roll music has played a great role in my life, often in ways which are subtle but by no means insignificant. Rock has been the cultural *lingua franca* of the past two or three generations of Americans, a fact which cultural elitists snidely disdain and which the media mercilessly exploits. But I'm sure that I am not alone when I confess that listening to rock and roll music started the process which made me become a poet. My first understanding of what poetry could do came around 1970, when I wore out LPs of Bob Dylan's *Highway 61 Revisited* and *Blonde on Blonde* albums. I have since worn out several additional LPs, eight-tracks, and cassettes of these same two albums, and am probably well on the way to wearing out my supposedly indestructible CDs. Rock and roll's influence on my life and thinking has been considerable. How could it not influence the forms and subjects of my poetry?

"'Buddy Holly' came about much in the way the poem suggests—a newspaper account reporting the discovery of Buddy Holly's shattered glasses in an Iowa morgue. 'Song of the Burning,' the Jim Morrison monologue, dates from several years before the wretched Oliver Stone movie, but the poem succumbs to the same sorts of glamorizing of its rather pathetic subject. The last few lines are loosely adapted from Mayakovsky's final poem/suicide note. I don't much care for the poem anymore. The remaining three poems in the selection are drawn from *Mystery Train,* a sequence in forty-five sections,

mainly sonnets, which attempts to use rock and roll music as a some-
what oddly refracted mirror of recent American history. To the best
of my knowledge, William Carlos Williams made no recorded state-
ments about Elvis, but the King surely illustrates the truth of Williams's
statement that 'the pure products of America go crazy.' Williams also
said the sonnet is a 'fascist form.' I have some fun with that statement
in the poem, for though the poem has the look of a late Williams
poem, it's in fact a couplet sonnet. The other two selections from
Mystery Train, 'Necromancy: The Last Days of Brian Jones' and 'Woody
Guthrie Visited by Bob Dylan . . .' are based upon actual incidents,
whose ironies, both funny and savage, were in keeping with the
sequence's themes. Sometimes I think that rock and roll is less a
cultural and artistic phenomenon than an allegory for the conse-
quences of fame and power, stories for which there are very few happy
endings."

BARON WORMSER, author of three books of poetry, lives in Mercer,
Maine.
"It all happened so fast."

ROBERT WRIGLEY's collections of poetry include *The Sinking of Clay
City, Moon in a Mason Jar,* and *What My Father Believed.* Winner of the
1988 Frederick Bock Award from *Poetry,* he lives at Omega Bend,
near Rattlesnake Point, on the Clearwater River, in Idaho.
"Rock and roll changes, rock and roll stays the same. In my youth, rock
was respite for me, a holy place, the hole in the wall. A comfortable
oblivion, rock was, for me, the haven of innocence I spent my last
summer in, before I was drafted in 1971 ('For the Last Summer'). It
was, as well, the doorway into the forbidden, where the flesh lived
happily and the only *then* was *now* ('The Prophecy'). It was a good
contradiction, a lovely ambiguity, an honest-to-god sweet nothing; in
this regard, rock was to me then what poetry is to me now—a way of
understanding and celebrating the human condition."

PAUL ZARZYSKI turned his rock and roll years into rock and rowel
when he moved, in the early seventies, from Wisconsin to Montana,
where he studied poetry with Richard Hugo and rode bucking horses
for a decade on the rodeo circuit. He has published two full collections

of poems, *The Make-Up of Ice* and *Roughstock Sonnets*. Today he makes his living reading and reciting his work in both the literati and *lari*ati arenas.

"The Vietnam era occurred in the midst of rock's heyday—in my opinion, that is—and in the middle of that time, fell my tumultuous, convoluted, pubescent youth, kind of a war *within* a war. From the PT boat waterskiing scene to 'I Can't Get No Satisfaction,' in the movie *Apocalypse Now,* to the backdrop music for a dozen other Nam films (that TV series, which I can't put a title to right now, used 'Paint It Black' as its theme song), to the powerful Kent Anderson novel titled *Sympathy for the Devil,* the music of the Rolling Stones seems most often associated with imagery of the Vietnam War. Simply put, rock and roll had more than a little to do with bringing 'home' to those of us in Vietnam, as well as bringing Vietnam to those of us at home."

Acknowledgments

The editor would like to thank Cindy Avino, Terry Miles, and Doug Hettinger for their help in preparing the manuscript of this anthology and David A. Dean for proofreading it.

Every effort has been made to trace copyright for the poems included in this anthology. The editor gratefully acknowledges the following permissions.

Peter Balakian. "Rock 'n Roll" is used by permission of the poet.

Dorothy Barresi. "The Back-Up Singer," "How It Comes," "Late Summer News," "Nine of Clubs, Cleveland, Ohio," "Vacation, 1969," and "Venice Beach: Brief Song" are from *All of the Above*, by Dorothy Barresi. Copyright 1991 by Dorothy Barresi. Reprinted by permission of Beacon Press.

Charles Baxter. "The Purest Rage" is from *Imaginary Paintings and Other Poems*, by Charles Baxter. Copyright 1989 by Charles Baxter. Reprinted by permission of British-American Publishing.

Bruce Berger. "Salad Days" is used by permission of the poet.

Judith Berke. "Dancing to the Track Singers at the Nightclub" and "Fifties Rock Party, 1985" are used by permission of the poet.

Richard Blessing. "Elegy for Elvis" is from *A Closed Book: Poems*, by Richard Blessing. Copyright 1981 by Richard Blessing. Reprinted by permision of University of Washington Press.

David Bottoms. "Homage to Lester Flatt" first appeared in *Poetry*, copyright 1985 by The Modern Poetry Association. Reprinted by permission of the editor of *Poetry*.

Neal Bowers. "On the Elvis Mailing List" first appeared in *Zone 3* 2, no. 1 (Winter 1987). Reprinted by permission of *Zone 3*.

Van K. Brock. "Mary's Dream" and "Sphinx" first appeared in *Bulletin:*

John. Copyright 1980 by David St. John. Reprinted by permission of the poet.

Kevin Stein. "First Performance of the Rock 'n Roll Band *Puce Exit*" and "World without End" first appeared in *Poetry Northwest* (Summer 1993). Reprinted by permission of the editor of *Poetry Northwest*. "Upon Finding a Black Woman's Door Sprayed with Swastikas, I Tell Her This Story of Hands" is reprinted by permission of the poet.

Alison Stone. "*Rocket to Russia*" first appeared in *Poetry*. Copyright 1987 by The Modern Poetry Association. "Spofford Hall" first appeared in *Poetry*. Copyright 1987 by The Modern Poetry Association. Both are reprinted by permission of the editor of *Poetry*.

Susan Swartwout. "I Wannabe Your Queen" is used by permission of the poet.

David Trinidad. "*Meet the Supremes*" and "'Monday, Monday'" are from *Hand over Heart: Poems 1981–1988,* by David Trinidad. Copyright 1991 by David Trinidad. Reprinted by permission of the poet.

Judith Vollmer. "Nursing the Sunburn" and "Wildsisters Bar" are from *Level Green,* by Judith Vollmer. Copyright 1990 by Judith Vollmer. Reprinted by permission of the University of Wisconsin Press.

Ronald Wallace. "Smoking" is reprinted from *The Makings of Happiness,* by Ronald Wallace, by permission of the University of Pittsburgh Press. Copyright 1991 by Ronald Wallace. "Sound Systems" is used by permission of the poet.

Doyle Wesley Walls. "The Summer the Beatles Went Over Seven Minutes on a Single" first appeared in *The Blue Moon* 3, no. 1 (1990). Reprinted by permission of the poet.

Michael Waters. "*American Bandstand*" is from *Anniversary of the Air,* by Michael Waters. Copyright 1985 by Michael Waters. Reprinted by permission of Carnegie Mellon University Press. "The Burden Lifters" is from *The Burden Lifters,* by Michael Waters. Copyright 1989 by Michael Waters. Reprinted by permission of Carnegie Mellon University Press. "Christ at the Apollo, 1962" first appeared in *Missouri Review*. Reprinted by permission of the poet.

Warren Woessner. "Jungle Music" first appeared in *Pig Iron: Landscapes of the Mind,* no. 13 (1985), edited by Jim Villani. Reprinted by permission of Pig Iron Press.

David Wojahn. "Buddy Holly" is from *Ice House Lights,* by David Wojahn. Copyright 1982 by David Wojahn. Reprinted by permission of Yale Uni-

Author Index

Title Index

Index to First Lines

Jim Elledge, Associate Professor of English at Illinois State University, has published two collections of poetry, *Various Envies* and *Nothing Nice,* and four critical volumes, *Standing "Between the Dead and the Living": The Elegiac Technique of Wilfred Owen's War Poems, Frank O'Hara: To Be True to a City, Weldon Kees: A Critical Introduction,* and *James Dickey: A Bibliography, 1947–1974.* Formerly Assistant Editor of *Poetry,* he is currently Editor of *The Illinois Review.*